BEGINNING
THE
CHRISTIAN LIFE

'This book is full of humanity, colour and above all Bible wisdom. It wonderfully beckons us into a life of following Christ, and I really don't think there is a better guide to give to a new Christian.'

Rico Tice, Author, *Christianity Explored*

BEGINNING THE CHRISTIAN LIFE

Richard Bewes

CHRISTIAN FOCUS

Unless otherwise noted, Scripture quotations are taken from the
NEW AMERICAN STANDARD BIBLE®, 1960, 1962, 1963,
1968, 1971, 1972, 1973, 1975, 1977, 1995 by The Lockman
Foundation. Used by permission.

ISBN 1-84550-017-2

Copyright © Richard Bewes 2004

Published in 2004
by
Christian Focus Publications, Ltd
Geanies House, Fearn, Tain,
Ross-shire, IV20 1TW, Scotland

www.christianfocus.com

Cover Design by Alister MacInnes

Printed and bound by
AIT Norhaven, Denmark

Contents

INTRODUCTION

My maternal grandfather had a great fondness for art. It was only late in life that he switched from a mere nominal belief in Christ to a personal faith that he could call his own. He once commissioned an artist to paint a picture of a watermill. The aim was to illustrate, through the ever-rushing torrent, a parable of our life's passing opportunities, which – when gone – can never be reclaimed.

Our existence on this world opens up the possibility of knowing God, and so establishing our true relationship to the universe. How to ensure that such an unrepeatable opportunity does not, like swirling water, slip by? My grandfather's water-colour prompts the viewer with its reminder.

My sister now possesses the painting, and every time I have looked at it, I am directed to a poem by Sarah Doudney – on which the painting was originally based. Its words are inscribed all around the picture frame.

THE LESSON OF THE WATERMILL

1. *Leave no tender word unsaid;*
    Love, while life shall last!
    The mill will never grind
    with the water that has passed.

2. *And the proverb haunts my mind*
   like a spell that's cast.
   The mill will never grind
   with the water that has passed.

3. *Power, intellect and strength*
   may not, cannot, last;
   The mill will never grind
   with the water that has passed.

4. *Take this lesson to your heart,*
   Take, oh! hold it fast;
   The mill will never grind
   with the water that has passed.

This book is designed to help many who are in the process of embarking upon the Christian life, and developing it. It can be used for bedtime – or reading in an aeroplane. It may also find a use in any church's outreach follow-up, or as a handbook in its discipleship or confirmation groups.

And what about my other grandfather – on my father's side? His was a very different story! He actually gets into my first chapter. I wish you pleasant reading.

RICHARD BEWES
All Souls Church, 2004.

1

ETERNITY – IN A MOMENT OF TIME

The picture caught me, at fifteen years of age, staring sternly ahead, five rows up in a 750-strong youthful semi-circle. A motorised camera, perched on a swivel, whirred slowly around the entire assembly. *The school photograph*. I still have my copy; it's a yard wide.

"Keep still as the lens comes opposite you!" came the barked instructions.

"Are you going to smile?" asked Peter Dufour, on my left.

I shook my head. The general opinion was that those who smiled at the camera as it focused on them were irremediable drips. Even so, there was a certain tension about the whole exercise. How to look? How to react? For a split second you were to be in the lens – "So *that's* what you were like at fifteen!" Five long years were about to be frozen into a permanent record of your life – in a moment of time.

One Tuesday night, back in 1882, my grandpa, Tommy Bewes – then fourteen – was crammed, shoulder to shoulder, within a similar crowd. It was September

9

26th. He was facing, not a camera (though I have a faded snapshot of him as a teenager) – but a challenge of a different kind. The youngest of twelve children, Tommy was about to make a decision that would affect his whole family, generations down the line. Unaccompanied by any of his eleven brothers and sisters, he was sitting with hundreds of others in Plymouth's Drill Hall on England's south coast – to hear the world's most effective public preacher, D.L. Moody of Chicago.

While there were no photographs that night (for Moody detested photographers), nevertheless in the vast crowd Tommy felt himself directly confronted by the searching lens of the preacher's message on God's words to Adam in the Garden of Eden – *Where art thou?*

> *At the close of the sermon there was silent prayer, and as the hushed audience bowed their heads Mr Moody pleaded with those amongthem who desired prayer to stand up for a moment and then resume their seats*
> *(Western Morning News, September 27th, 1882).*

According to the newspaper, fifty-four people registered their decision for Jesus Christ that evening. "I am glad to see so many young men getting up," Moody was reported to declare. "They may have forty or fifty years of life before them, and what a great deal they can do for God in that time!"

Judging by the letter written the following Friday by Tommy – one of the fifty-four – the significance of the occasion had not been lost on the fourteen-year-old. The letter was addressed to his sister Evy, next up in the family line. We still possess it:

He spoke from the 9th verse of the 3rd of Genesis. It is Where art thou? He said that that was the 1st question that God ever asked in the Bible, and that it was the first question that people ought to ask themselves and he said that there were two more that he was going to speak about and they were, Where are you going? And How are you going to spend eternity? I don't think he could have chosen better ones.

It could have been only thirty or forty minutes-worth of listening for Tommy Bewes – but a great deal of Bible and mission emphasis in our family today can be traced back to that single address in the Drill Hall.

It happens all the time in the world of sport, politics or the arts – *seeing and seizing the key moment.* The scoring of the crucial goal that turns the match, the vital television interview that swings an election; the taking of the film role that launches a career.

But you can triumph in any of these arenas, yet still miss what the whole thing is about. Varro, the first century Roman poet, set about collecting people's opinions on the question, *What is the true object of human life?* He had no less than 320 different answers.

The contention of the Christian faith is that this is the big question. It concerns the establishing of our own relationship to the universe and its Creator; the working out of who we are and what we are here *for* on this, the only inhabited planet in all existence. It also relates to what the future holds for us, when our flickering lifespan is over – for a person with a poor view of the future, can never hope to make any proper sense of the present. All of this, then, comprised the mountainous issue that Tommy Bewes got sorted out in a single evening – culminating in,

How are you going to spend eternity?

But it is also a very simple issue. A fourteen-year-old can get it. My sister Elizabeth got it at the age of ten. It is so simple that some of the greatest intellects we ever produced have missed it. Many belief-systems are everlastingly occupied with humanity's *Long Search*! How and where is God to be found? But Christianity turns the exercise around completely with God's first question, 'Where art THOU?' *The reality is that from those earliest beginnings it is God who has been looking and searching for us.*

This is the story of the Bible, and Jesus is the clue to it all. He was predicted as far back as the Garden of Eden as the human 'offspring' who would reverse the effects of our human fall and crush the power of evil (Genesis 3:15). This second Person of the Trinity, in his pre-incarnate appearings and prophetic foreshadowings, haunts the pages of the Old Testament, until finally as a human baby he makes his historical appearance on the world stage as the God-Man Jesus Christ.

Once recognise this heartbeat of relationship and pursuing love at the centre of all things – *and the universe itself begins to glow with significance.* More times than I can possibly count, I have met with enquirers staying behind after a Christian meeting. I tell them that the Bible's message is an announcement!

- *First*, that God loves us – as people made in his image – desiring us to be in relationship with himself.

- *Second*, that since the early days of our human story, we have been out of relationship with our Creator, through our bid for independence. We have become an offence to him, have been banished from his presence, and are headed for a lost eternity – every one of us.

• *Third*, that the story of the Bible is of God's loving intervention in our condemned race. He has worked in history, and supremely through Jesus, to accept in himself the penalty of our rebellion, so bearing it instead of us. **This was done, once and for all time on the cross. There Jesus – who was both God and human – died for the sins (past, present and future) of the whole world. Our judgement has already been borne by God in Christ – who has been bodily raised from the dead as living Saviour for all time!**

• *Fourth*, that Christ – with his saving work done, and now resurrected and ascended – is to be received and followed personally as universal Saviour and Lord. For us to be restored to a right relationship with God, *there is nothing for us to do*, beyond **repenting** of the sins that kept him out of our lives and, in grateful prayer, **trusting** in Christ and his death for the forgiveness of our sins for time and eternity. As we receive him into our lives, his Spirit comes to indwell us, bringing us Christ's friendship and equipping us to serve him boldly and openly for the rest of our days – and with eternity to come.

'**How are you going to spend eternity?**' The question can only be answered satisfactorily when the relationship to Christ has been established. Do we have to wait until we die, to discover whether or not we have been accepted by God? *The answer is No.* In Plymouth's Drill Hall, fourteen-year-old Tommy came to realise that eternity for him had been settled there and then – in that moment of time.

But is it really admissable that the entire story of what I am in the next life should depend upon a split-second response in this life to the love of God in the death of Jesus? The answer is that our life on this strange blue-green planet passes so quickly that it may be seen as a succession of decisions compressed into a single 'Yes' or 'No' about Jesus Christ. Alexsander Solzhenitsyn wrote, *Only one life is allotted us, one small, short life.* I heard an after-dinner speech from the American evangelist, Billy Graham, in London's Guildhall. He confided that in all his long ministry his greatest surprise had been 'the brevity of life'.

Our so-short life will finally be assessed as a single decision – and it passes all too quickly. True, there can be last-minute 'death-bed repentances'. We can rightly instance the example of the thief, dying on the cross next to Jesus. His gasping prayer for the Lord to 'remember' him – uttered at the tail end of a disreputable life – was honoured; he would indeed be admitted to Paradise.

But as a Christian minister I have been with many people on their death-beds; they run into hundreds. *The unbelievers among them who turn in faith to Christ at the last moment can be numbered on the fingers of one hand.* One modern reason is obvious; by the time you are on your death-bed you are likely to be pumped so full of drugs that you will be in no state to decide what you are going to have for dinner, let alone how you are going to spend eternity.

The decision for Christ that sums up a whole lifetime, then, is surely to be made at the earliest opportunity! The New Testament makes no promises for tomorrow. It states the issue clearly and starkly:

> *As God's fellow-workers we urge you not to receive God's grace in vain. For he says, "In the time of my favour I heard you, and in the day of salvation I helped you." I tell you, now is the time of God's favour, now is the day of salvation* (2 Corinthians 6:1,2).

The implication of these words is that they were addressed to readers who already had some relationship with the Christian faith. God's searching camera lens swivels around the church just as much as it does through secular society. There is a mass of people – in nodding acquaintance with the message of the Cross and Resurrection – who never close the deal to become followers of Jesus. These are the drifters in and out of church; they are the fellowship of the uncommitted.

It was so in Christ's days by the Sea of Galilee. The religious authorities at that time failed to see that they were living at the very parting of history; it was left to the common people to recognise that the time of their opportunity was upon them.

If your senses are alert you can tell when something is happening. "What's going on?" Liz and I once asked a London policeman. We were crossing Portland Place, where an obvious build-up of security was taking place.

"*It's Maggie,*" came the reply. "she'll be here in five minutes." The former Prime Minister was about to descend on the Chinese embassy.

Open the pages of the New Testament, as the camera lens swivels from one locality to another. What's happening?

"Jesus of Nazareth is passing by", a blind man was told, as the crowd pressed around him outside Jericho. The chance had to be grabbed, with shouts for help, and the carpenter-preacher – on his way to achieve the redemption of the world – was stopped in his tracks to bring healing and salvation, to a solitary individual.

Minutes later it was the turn of Zacchaeus, a despised, grubby tax-collector – up one of the trees that lined the high street, hoping for a better view. Suddenly the lens is on him, as Jericho's visitor looks up into the tree. "Zacchaeus, come down immediately. I must stay at your house today" (Luke 19:5). It's now or never for Zacchaeus, for Christ never came to Jericho again. But the challenge was accepted, and a man's life was irrevocably changed: "Today, salvation has come to this house!" declared Jesus.

Whether it was an afflicted woman, squeezing through a crowd to touch his clothes, or an enquiring Pharisee coming by night to avoid unwelcome publicity, the Gospels are not short of stories in which men and women recognised their moment of opportunity with Jesus of Nazareth – and took it.

There was urgency in these accounts, and it must be added that there was a sense of urgency in the mind of Jesus too. "I have a baptism to be baptised with," he once said, as he referred to his coming death, "and how I am constrained until it is accomplished!" The future destiny of millions was to hang upon that single event. The Cross, then, was to pinpoint for Jesus himself the same theme – of eternity, in a moment of time. His life and ministry have split the dispensations into BC and AD.

If anything, the sense of urgency increased after Christ's ascension, as the early Christian witness began to fan out onto 58,000 miles of Roman trunk roads with the story of new life in Christ – the winner over death and hell. Peace with God for ever, forgiveness full and free, eternal life as a gift; Never mind the flames of persecution and martyrdom, the good news was too momentous to suppress!

Around the world, as I write, up to 100,000 new believers every day are being added to the fellowship of Christ's followers. *If you are not one already, will you become one now?* Each week some 1,600 new congregations are coming into being; churches that were not in existence before. For every African baby being born on the African continent today, two Africans are becoming Christians. In Brazil, too, the numbers of new believers in Christ are outstripping the birthrate. During the decade that straddled the new millennium, Britain – for all its secularism – witnessed a membership increase of sixty-eight percent in those churches where the Scriptures are steadily and systematically taught. This was certainly happening in our church of All Souls, Langham Place.

These facts will no more hit the popular headlines today than did those indomitable Christians at the time of the Roman Caesars. Then, as now, if it wasn't the threat of Barbarians and terrorism on the border, it was the social whirl of the circus, the sports arena or the latest popular celebrity that captured the public attention.

But the real story was taking place all the time, largely out of sight. Augustine of Carthage described the phenomenon, back in the fifth century: "One loving spirit sets another on fire." Every story of coming to faith in Christ is

17

different… but there is usually a friend somewhere in the background – encouraging, praying, discussing. These Christian friends would like to make the great decision for us! But that can never be.

At some point, the message of the cross – where Jesus died for your sins – comes into view, while you for your part are held in God's viewfinder, transfixed in a moment of time. Eternity opens up before you, and a voice behind the lens seems to be saying, "Turn and believe. I tell you, now is the time of God's favour, now is the day of salvation."

* * * * *

I am getting into a quiet place. This is my moment to receive Christ as Saviour and Lord. But…. had I, however tentatively, made such a decision before? In that case I can firm it up, writing over in ink what has, perhaps, only been written in pencil so far. And will he come into my life if I ask him? Yes, he says he will:

"Behold, I stand at the door and knock. If anyone hears my voice and opens the door, I will come in to him and eat with him and he with me" (Revelation 3:20).

LORD JESUS CHRIST, I DESIRE WITH ALL MY HEART TO BE ONE OF THE MANY WHO, AROUND THE WORLD THIS DAY, ARE ACCEPTING YOU INTO THEIR LIVES. I RECOGNISE YOU AS TRUE GOD OF MY LIFE. FORGIVE ME FOR MY SINS, AND FOR LEAVING YOU OUT OF MY LIFE UNTIL NOW. THANK YOU FOR DYING FOR ME UPON THE CROSS. IN THIS MOMENT I AM TRUSTING

YOU FOR TIME AND ETERNITY. COME INTO MY LIFE, LORD JESUS, AND I WILL ACKNOWLEDGE YOU AS MY SAVIOUR AND LORD FROM NOW ON. AMEN.

I snuggled down under the blankets. Yes, it had been *my* decision those years ago. Like my grandpa before me I had been in my teens when I made it. There had been about a hundred of us, listening to Mr Nash of the Scripture Union as he spoke about the Christ who knocks at the door of our lives. *I am going to do what that man at the front is saying*, I silently resolved. The meeting concluded and banter and talk took over…. but nothing was going to stop me. It was the moment for me, and later – sitting up in bed – I prayed my prayer of commitment. Tomorrow morning I would wake up to a new day of adventure on Planet Earth – with the Lord Jesus Christ!

2

THE MORNING AFTER

"And now for a Tom and Jerry colour cartoon!"

A cheer went up from a hundred and fifty girls and boys, crammed one December evening into Emmanuel Church Hall, in the London suburb of Northwood. It was an international Christmas party, and the room was alight with enthusiasm. I watched as my colleague, the Rev Alex Ross, confidently pressed the projector switch. The lights dimmed.

Anticlimax.... something was wrong! I froze in my seat. A mix-up. The agency had delivered the wrong film to Alex. *Groan*! Instead of Tom and Jerry in colour, we were watching a black-and-white documentary on the British seaweed industry!

Maybe you think that the Christian package turns out the same way. All those promises about the new life of receiving Christ. The colour and joy about forgiveness and resurrection. Then I wake up to a monochrome Monday morning – back to the old familiar world, where yesterday's great decision seems a million miles away. Had I been conned by my feelings? True, I'd made a decision about Jesus, and thought I'd solved the biggest problem in my life. Now it appears my problems have doubled! *If only my family and friends understood, and if only I wasn't such a horrible person. How could I ever be part of all that church stuff; why am I so aware of my failings, and why do I feel that I'm in No Man's Land? Did I get it wrong? Had I better start all over again?*

To feel this way as a new Christian is not a bad sign at all; so often it is the sure-fire indication that someone has genuinely changed sides, and crossed the border into uncomfortably new territory – which is none other than the eternal kingdom of God! New problems there may be, but they are as nothing compared to the blockbuster problem that God has dealt with once and for all in the life of every one of his newest followers:

> *He has delivered us from the domain of darkness and transferred us to the kingdom of his beloved Son, in whom we have redemption, the forgiveness of sins (Colossians 1:13,14).*

However, the new believer is like a visitor to a strange country. Everything seems novel and challenging. Why, just crossing over to France can be a hair-raising experience in itself. To find yourself, as Liz and I once did, on an unlit road, halfway up a mountain, driving on the 'wrong' side of the road at dead of night; my wife being obliged to use the gear lever on the other side of an unfamiliar hired car, semi-tropical rain beating against the windscreen, the windows completely steamed up. My allotted role – with the help of a failing torch – was to follow the directions that had been laboriously hand-written in *French*! Somehow we made it.

It is no less confusing for some Christian beginners. An unfamiliar guide book, the Bible; strange travelling-companions in the Christian Church; the oddest music you ever heard, and a strange new vocabulary of 'forgiveness', 'grace', 'prayer', 'fellowship' and 'the Spirit'. On top of that are the temptations and trials that test a new-found faith; battles and upsets, doubts and set-backs.

"So how do I know that I'm a Christian?" Many followers of Jesus exist for too long in the mists of uncertainty, but that is not what is intended for us! Not according to the Scriptures. Here is Christ's closest disciple, John:

> *"I write these things to you who believe in the name of the Son of God so that you may know that you have eternal life"* *(1 John 5:13).*

It is not smug self-satisfaction or presumption to know that we are already possessors of eternal life, here and now. After all, it is not we but *Christ* who gained this cyclonic achievement for us by the death that he died; the credit is his, and his alone. All we had to do was to thank him and accept the gift. We are *allowed* to know of our eternal security. He desires it for every one of those who trust him for their eternal salvation. More than that; God has provided three massive ways of strengthening the Christian's confidence. The first is the Word of God itself:

The Word of God

After all, it was God's revealed truth – the Bible – that started this whole business off! It is in grasping its life-changing message that millions of us have received Christ at all. So it is to the Bible that I must turn as a new believer, if I am to find any firm assurance that God actually *did* something in me and for me, when I turned in faith to his Son, Jesus. My *feelings* will be a far less reliable barometer of my spiritual standing, for emotions can be deceptive. They will fluctuate with the weather, with the success of the new diet, with the latest developments in the shares index! Everything else may change around us, but the Scriptures have stood up against the batterings of many centuries.

The newest, most timid Christian recruit can cling like a limpet to God's promises from the start. What promises are we talking about? The New Testament is brimming with them.

But to all who did receive him, who believed in his name, he gave the right to become children of God (John 1:12).

Whoever comes to me I will never cast out (John 6:37).

And this is the testimony, that God gave us eternal life, and this life is in his Son. Whoever has the Son has life; whoever does not have the Son of God does not have life (1 John 5:11,12).

Behold, I stand at the door and knock. If anyone hears my voice and opens the door, I will come in to him and eat with him and he with me (Revelation 3:20).

"Has Christ come into your life?" I once asked a student.

"Er, well, I hope so."

"Did you pray the prayer, asking him to come into your life?"

"Oh yes, I did this evening."

"Have a look, then, and see what he promises to anyone who opens the door to him. *I will come in*. So you opened the door?"

"Yes, yes."

"Then did he come into your life?"

"I suppose he must have!"

"What makes you so sure?"

"Well, *because he says he will*. Okay, I see it now!"

Coming to Christ or Christ coming to me? Me being 'in Christ' as the New Testament puts it, or Christ being 'in' me? Actually it amounts to the same thing. Throw a sponge into the bathwater! Is the water in the sponge or the sponge in the water? Both are true. When I come to Christ and receive him into my life, the result is that I belong to him for ever, and he belongs to me. *It says so in the Scriptures.*

Here is a sure and safe ground of Christian assurance – the Bible. Neglect it, and uncertainties crowd in. Attend to it, and a firm platform begins to grow under our feet. We will learn more about this Book of books in a couple of chapters. But come now to a second signpost that the newest follower of Christ has been accepted:

The Work of Christ

It is the *saving* work of Christ – through his death on the cross – that his disciples rely upon completely for their eternal forgiveness. We contribute nothing; he has done it all. But why couldn't Jesus simply die for us in bed? *Reason:* The cross represents the very worst that human beings can do to a person. The fact that we can do it to the Son of God says it all. The cry was not, *Exclude him* *from temple worship....Incarcerate him in prison....*or even – as happened to Socrates of ancient Greece – *Give him poison to drink.* At the very least, Socrates died in dignity, chatting amiably with his friends as he swallowed the hemlock.

Not so with the Son of God. The hatred of the whole rebellious human race against divine love is summed up by the infectious cry that has crossed the centuries, *Let him be crucified!* 'It is the most cruel and shameful of all punishments,' Cicero had observed, a generation earlier. 'Let it never come near the body of a Roman citizen, nay, neither near his thoughts or eyes or ears.' The cross exposed in full the nature of human sin.

The mocking, the spitting, the buffeting, the scourging, the stripping, the agony of the nails, the burning heat of the sun, the thirst, the flies, the desolation; and death by slow asphyxiation – in full exposure to jeering onlookers, laughing as you die – this accurately describes humanity's basic response to the sovereign Lord. "Look at this 'King' now!" was the taunt.

Millions *have* looked, and millions have been transformed by the look. *Did we really do that?* But look further! For if the cross represented the worst that humans could do, it simultaneously demonstrated the best that God could do in Christ – not only in receiving the full blows of our hatred summed up by the terrible Roman cross, but in accepting the responsibility for the offence that we are to God – the penalty of which is banishment and rejection from heaven. This, too, was taking place in the death of Jesus. Christ was "killed by the hands of lawless men", but – amazingly – it also happened "according to the definite plan and foreknowledge of God" (Acts 2:23).

And the resurrection of Christ was the public, divine endorsement of what he had achieved.

There, outside Jerusalem, God in Christ had been intercepting his own judgement upon the human race. On the cross Jesus was suspended between heaven and earth. Earth was quite clearly rejecting him – *but heaven was also*. The sky went dark, and a cry of dereliction went up, 'My God, my God, why have you forsaken me?' It was a direct quotation from Psalm 22, and therefore a fulfilment of prophecy. The implications are starkly clear: Christ, the God-Man – the only pure being who has ever lived – was enduring the very judgement of hell and banishment that we deserved, in our place and as our Substitute. At that moment in space, time and history, *He* was the offender – the cheat, the fraudster, the sexual offender, the slanderer. Our banishment had become his. No one could possibly have done this for us, but God in human form. John Chrysostom, the mighty Christian preacher and theologian of the fourth century, expressed this stark truth of what theologians call 'penal substitution': "God was about to punish them; this he did not do. They were about to perish, but he gave his own Son *instead of them.*"

The result is that we are off the hook, for ever, as we gratefully accept what he has done for us freely. It is the only way of forgiveness, for – as Jesus anticipated his suffering – he had prayed, "If it be possible let this cup pass from me. Nevertheless not my will, but yours be done." But it was not to be. If there had been any other way by which we could have been forgiven, Christ would never have died that death. But he has done so – here is the historical demonstration that I *am* forgiven, as someone who has accepted him. **If he endured so much to remove the judgement that I have deserved – why, of course he has forgiven me; it would be an insult to him if I thought otherwise!**

The shameful cross, pronounced Cicero of Roman times. *The Wondrous Cross*, wrote hymn writer Isaac Watts of Southampton, seventeen centuries later. How do I know I am forgiven and accepted, then? This second signpost points to the work of Christ for us. But there is a further undergirding of the Christian's security:

The Witness of the Holy Spirit

This is something inward, of which we read in the New Testament:

> *The Spirit himself bears witness with our spirit that we are children of God, and if children, then heirs – heirs of God and fellow-heirs with Christ, provided we suffer with him in order that we may also be glorified with him (Romans 8:16,17).*

Here the apostle Paul is writing to Christian believers. "But," we may argue, "this begins to sound as though my Christian confidence does have to do with my 'feelings' after all."

Not exactly. It is more to do with *experience*, the growing experience of Christ's transforming Spirit in my character, outlook and lifestyle. Some changes begin to make themselves apparent when Christ moves in!

What has happened is this. When people receive Christ as Saviour and Lord, they will often say, "I have accepted Christ into my life." They are quite right in saying this. But technically what took place was that *the Spirit of Christ* (yes, he is a Person) came to indwell life and personality. The Spirit of Christ – or 'The Holy Spirit' as the Scriptures describe him – is given to us from Day One of our coming to accept the Lord.

He is the third Person of the Trinity; he has been there for all of eternity and is part of the very Godhead that has been at work for our forgiveness and salvation. It is a stupendous realisation that the three divine Persons of the Trinity act together, though in different ways, for our permanent safety:

- The Father **authorised** our salvation, *eternally*, in his loving plans
- The Son **achieved** our salvation, *historically*, by his willing death
- The Spirit **activated** our salvation *personally*, as we trusted in Christ

Jesus informed his disciples that after his bodily departure from the world, the Holy Spirit – 'another Counsellor' – would come and indwell his friends (John 14:16-18). Not a *different* Counsellor, but, a second Counsellor or 'Helper'. The Holy Spirit would make the unseen presence and friendship of Jesus a reality to believers worldwide.

We must explore this further in a later chapter, but an illustration may help. A returning sports champion is triumphantly coming down the aeroplane gangway at London Heathrow Airport. Several hundred fans have turned up – just for a glimpse; if they're lucky they might even get a handshake. However, the heady experience is disappointingly short-lived; after only a few minutes the celebrity is driven away in a car. But later that evening comes the explanation. There on screen, in the TV studio, is the same familiar figure – but now made accessible, not simply to a few, but to literally millions of devotees, by this 'other' medium.

So with the Spirit. *Jesus left this world bodily, taken away from the few, in order to become accessible to the many*, to believers on every continent of the world. By the ministry of this 'other' Counsellor – the Holy Spirit – the very presence of Christ can be with you in your one-room apartment and (better than a sports personality) right in your very heart and life. The Spirit is not given to draw attention to himself, so much as to make Jesus real to us. This awareness of Jesus brings certain changes!

Do we find ourselves beginning to respond to Christ's leadership, so that we want to please him? Do we begin to sense an affinity with others who belong to him? Are we increasingly aware of hostile pressure from those who reject his claims? Is the Bible beginning to light up our understanding? Are we, however feebly, conscious of a new battle – against temptation and low standards? Does it now hurt us when we hear Christ and his church being spoken against?

If the answer to some of these questions is Yes, then take heart; you already have something of the witness of the Spirit within you!

Even suffering for our beliefs is a valid experience of the Spirit's work in our lives. So we learn from the passage quoted earlier, Romans 8:16,17. What has happened is that we have turned around and are swimming against the current of so many established prejudices and accepted standards. There may be pressure – *but the pressure itself is a reassurance.*

We will have taken on board by now that the three Persons of the divine Trinity combine together to help the believer onto a firm platform of humble confidence that we are indeed Christ's person for ever. The Word of God, the Work of the Son and the Witness of the Holy Spirit are given to tell the timid beginner, 'Yes, you've started; you are on the road.'

The love of Christ in your life; is it there, however faint and flickering? If so, something has happened that the cleverest sages of old failed to get hold of. Even the mighty Aristotle, born four centuries before Christ, once remarked, "It would sound odd for a man to say he loved a god."

But millions of us do! How to develop and strengthen that love? We'll hold that for the next chapter.

3

'A BELIEVER IS
SURELY A LOVER'

In the very middle of Italy a little boy was born in the year AD 342, at a place called Strido. His name was Jerome. He was destined to become a renowned scholar, specialising in the works of the great Cicero. But something happened, that changed the entire course of his life.

Jerome dreamt that he had died and duly arrived at the gates of heaven.

"Who are you?" demanded the gatekeeper.

"*Christianus sum*", replied the applicant. "I'm a Christian."

"No!" came the retort. "*Ciceronianus es, non Christianus!*" "You're a Ciceronian; not a Christian! You see," said the gatekeeper, "here we judge people by what they were most, when they lived their life below. And you devoted your whole life to the classics and the works of Cicero, and neglected the things of God and the Scriptures. So we judge you not to be a Christian, but a Ciceronian. Sorry!"

Jerome woke in a sweat, and made his resolve there and then. *I will be a Christian. I will follow the teaching of Christ and the Scriptures.* Jerome rose to become the greatest of all scholars in the early church – but with a difference. Christ was now the centre of his love and loyalty, and the Bible the object of his chief study. From the Hebrew and the Greek he translated the Bible into Latin, the common language used across all Europe. His version was called the Vulgate. It lasted the Continent for a thousand years.

What are you most? I think of a monthly professional breakfast party, hosted in London across many years by the Bible teacher John Stott. Looking around, could one tick off what the guests were into? Easy! Law, psychiatry, politics, media or business. But none of those professions represented what any of the guests were *most*. No. Once the coffee and toast were cleared away, Bibles would be pulled out. A time of prayer would be held. The whole purpose was to strengthen each other's *shared love of Christ*. That was the great essential that described every person in the room.

Soren Kierkegaard of Denmark put it well in 1849:

A believer is surely a lover; yea, of all lovers the most in love! [1]

The test of what someone is most is likely to arise when adversity strikes; when either status or work – thought by so many to define identity – have been removed; when ill health takes over and personal props are knocked away or – as happens in many countries – when terrorism or a coup threaten basic stability. "When they come for you at night," wrote an East African family friend, "and threaten

---

[1] *The Sickness Unto Death* (Doubleday Anchor Books, 1955 edition, p.234).

to tie a sack over your head and drop you in the river, then you know whether Jesus means everything to you, or whether he means nothing at all."

I was interviewing John Stott in a public meeting.

"What are you looking forward to, more than anything else, John?"
"I think," came the reply, "I can honestly say that, above everything else, I'm looking forward to becoming more like Jesus Christ."

If such a thing is happening – is beginning to happen – or even if we are simply *hungry* for it to happen to us – then it can be said that, regardless of every circumstance or personal adversity – **we are fulfilling the purpose for which we were born!** By comparison, nothing else matters. The apostle Paul knew this. Confined to jail, yet aspiring to know Christ better, he was able to affirm,

"I have learnt to be content, whatever the circumstances" (*Philippians 4:11*).

How then to develop into what we wish to be most, a 'lover' of Christ?

What do lovers do? *They like to spend time with each other.* Yes, of course we may see it as a disadvantage that Christ is invisible to us. How to love someone we cannot see? But this is where the miracle of the gift of the Holy Spirit has stretched across the centuries. In speaking of Christ, the apostle Peter could have been writing to Christians today when he addressed those scattered, persecuted believers of his own time:

> *Though you have not seen him, you love him; and even though you do not see him now, you believe in him and are filled with an inexpressible and glorious joy, for you are receiving the goal of your faith, the salvation of your souls (1 Peter 1:8,9).*

"Oh, I love Jesus so much!" I heard a Romanian exclaim in the city of Oradea. But why? We had just been holding a Bible study there. It was not the Bible expositor who was the object of such love – nor even the Bible in itself – but the Person to whom the Bible was directing us all, as we shared Christ together in a crowded church. It was standing room only, for a good half of the assembled company. *He* was the magnet.

There was evidently great hunger in that community for the Bible – and for the Lord of which it spoke. Many of the people there had no Bibles of their own; thus a great deal of the Bible intake had to be of a corporate nature. There was also united prayer together at dawn every single day. *People would come by the hundred.* A corporate daily 'Quiet Time'!

They must often have done it like this in the early days of the Christian church – when people possessed no Bibles of their own, when indeed the New Testament had yet to be written down. The local leaders would unravel a scroll from the apostle Paul, and read it to the gathered Christians. They would pray, they would worship and they would exult in what they heard – and then fan out into their community in bold witness.

There is a great deal to be said for 'meeting together' and so to 'encourage one another' (Hebrews 10:25). Sunday is an obvious example, and weekends away together provide extra opportunity. A threesome, or a one-on-one can be powerful in its effectiveness. **However, nothing can quite replace the secret meeting of a believer, alone with God.**

This is to be understood as a delight, not as a legal requirement or useful technique. The Christian life is a relationship. What relationship ever needed a technique for its success? Yet lovers still need an arrangement.

"We'll meet at the Washington Memorial this afternoon."

"Look for me at Eros Statue in Piccadilly tonight!"

"See you in Nairobi at the Thorn Tree restaurant next week!"

We can do the same and establish that rendezvous with the Lord every day. It's an exciting prospect – where will it be? And when? *Arrange it with Him*. The place.... the time – even if it can only be a grabbed precious ten-minutes. Sometimes, when at a conference centre I've done it by the tennis court – early, before the waking first bird-like call of some tennis freak breaks the stillness! A bit of Bible, some application; then talk to the Lord, and off into breakfast. I've seen people do it – their Bibles open – in parks, on buses and on subway trains.

It's basically two questions we are answering as we meet with our unseen companion. *Firstly*: What am I going to learn about the Lord today? And *secondly*: Having learnt it, How can I please Him today? For I have – in the prospect of the next twelve hours and more – a new fresh day of adventure with Jesus Christ! So I ask for the privilege of walking beside Him as his loving, faithful helper. Whom will I meet today? What's going to happen? Let me be filled with his Spirit here and now!

I must be honest; when it comes to suitable venues, *there isn't usually a tennis court on hand for me*. It could even be raining. And as a matter of fact, I have found that certain surroundings can distract me from the very purpose of my rendezvous, which is to focus my love and loyalty on Christ. So, as a general pattern, the bedroom can be as good a meeting place as any. The meeting can even begin ahead of schedule. Lying on your bed – your eyes slowly opening, as you condition your reflexes for the day ahead, with the film of the day's plans beginning to roll on the screen of your mind – you're silently saying, "Another day of adventure on Planet Earth….and I want it to be for you."

A cup of tea? Up, into the bathroom *next*, and *then* the meeting with the Lord…. or the other way round? And *must* it be morning, or could it be at bedtime? Or both? Or the middle of the day, even? Or on the train? And what if there's a lively family to be got up and given breakfast? Let alone dinner, tea and bathtime for the kids! Work it out. *Arrange it with Him*. However, for many people the words of the nineteenth-century American clergyman Henry Ward Beecher make plenty of sense:

> *The first hour of waking is the rudder that guides the whole day.*

Not that you are obliged to fill a whole hour with the Bible and prayer. Start with ten minutes, and see if your appetite grows. What are you going to read? A psalm? One of the four Gospels? Why not begin with Luke – written by a Gentile for Gentile readers, and see if these teeming stories about Jesus don't put a glow into your heart?

The Bible is now open before you. A prayer for understanding, in echo of the psalmist David: 'Open my eyes, that I may behold wonderful things out of your Law.' And then…. just read! It may only be a couple of paragraphs. It could be a whole chapter. But as you read, you are expecting to find God's message for yourself that very day….

What *bit* of the reading are you now going to take into the day? What did you like best? That episode? No. That verse? N-n-no. But – maybe, this bit…. about Jesus' attitude to his enemies. *Lord, help me to learn from the way you faced your critics.*

There you are; already your reading is turning into praying. God's word came to you in the Bible; now you're speaking back to Him in prayer. Why not start with praise for a new day and thanksgiving for what you've read? Is there something that's been wrong that you want to put right with Him? And then…. intercession; that's *asking*. Try praying on the fingers of one hand. *The thumb first*; that's the finger closest to me – so I remember family members and cherished friends. *The forefinger* next; that's the pointing, 'directing' finger – so I bring to the Lord those who have authority over me in some way: my boss, my teachers, our church leadership. And next? Why, that's *the big, the prominent finger* – so I bring into my prayers Heads of State and the political authorities as they wrestle with today's world issues. Then I can add to them the church leaders worldwide, together with evangelists and missionaries proclaiming Christ's message; in a dying world no-one can be more important than them.

Then comes *the fourth finger*; pianists call this the 'weak' finger. This reminds me to remember the sick and those who minister to them; children in need, the disadvantaged and the homeless of our cities. But I also remember those known to me in the greatest need of all – people without the knowledge of Christ – whom I long will share my faith one day. And last of all? *The little finger*; that's me of course, with my hopes, my problems and opportunities….and the day ahead!

And what was that bit from Luke? I'll murmur it to myself as I go out of the door. Maybe it'll surface later and enable me at some point to lift my thoughts once more to this invisible, yet ever-present Lord with whom my day is being shared.

The *Quiet Time*; your agreed secret rendezvous with the Master of the Universe!

Jeremiah, the prophet of old found it was as good as a breakfast. 'When your words came, I ate them; they were my joy and my heart's delight' (Jeremiah 15:16). *David* the psalmist opted for a morning arrangement: 'I rise before dawn and cry for help. I have put my hope in your word' (Psalm 119:147). *Isaiah* also liked the morning: 'The sovereign Lord has given me an instructed tongue, to know the word that sustains the weary. He wakens me morning by morning, wakens my ear to listen like one being taught' (Isaiah 50:4).

The impression given is of a regular habit – and the focus is upon God and his Word. *Let it always be the Bible*. There will be other books of devotion and spiritual encouragement that can feed and instruct us, but for your secret rendezvous, let it be the primary documents themselves that give shape to your life day by day.

Are you new in your discipleship, wondering what books of the Bible you are meant to read? Read them all! But kick off with Luke. Then as the idea of a settled arranged time begins to take hold, get advice from your local church leaders; there are likely to be available various Bible reading schemes and explanatory notes, to help Christian readers develop into what God has wanted from all eternity – *people in love with his Son Jesus Christ!*

4

A CAN OF COKE AND SOME BIBLES

"Okay, Bibles away – let's see who wants to book a practice court for tomorrow morning!"

We were at Iona Birchall's house in Wimbledon. She and her husband Mark had put on a barbecue for some of the players, on the eve of the world's greatest tennis championships. Even Americans, rightly proud of their great tournament at Flushing Meadow, New York, still call those two weeks at Wimbledon 'The Big W'.

And there was I – at Iona and Mark's invitation – to do Bible study with some of the best players in the world. It was rather an honour. Two things interested me. First – how much some of these players could put away, and still keep slim! Liz and I would observe the same phenomenon at our own home when players came back after a Sunday 'tennis outreach service' at church. These things can sometimes be done if your church is in a big capital city.

"Let me just warn you, Richard," I remember being advised by the Americans' travelling tennis chaplain, "Sandy likes to eat a lot".

"A lot?" I queried. "A lot of what, exactly?"

"*Anything*," came the reply.

And so it proved. It was all burned off the next day in a quarter final on the Centre Court.

Now it was the same at the barbecue. The Birchalls had done the players proud.

The second thing that interested me was the sheer brevity of it all. The players piled in for the food. When it was over we did about twenty minutes' Bible study together, followed by five or six minutes of prayer – and suddenly it was over. Anyone want a practice court?

These are action men and women, I reflected. It probably has to be like that, when you're a believer on the move, in a different city every week and living out of a suitcase. You grab what opportunities you can, for fellowship and church, and the building of your life as a Christian. Without such get-togethers – however brief – your inner life can shrivel.

It's at the close level of a small group that the big lessons, learnt in the wider teaching of overall church worship, need to be put into practice. 'Bear with each other,' Christians are told, 'and forgive whatever grievances you may have against one another' (Colossians 3:13). But how is that ever done? *It happens in the small group context*, where we get to know each other's faults and personal needs at close quarters.

Barbecues and their like can help the Christian who is on the move – to some extent. But on the local scene **it is the mushrooming of thousands of small groups worldwide that has been a remarkable feature of church growth in the last few decades.** Such groups can be set up for people exploring the Christian faith for the first time, for beginners who have made the great decision to follow Christ and wish to grow, for students who need to meet with each other on an equal level – and for well-established believers looking for regular fellowship around the study of the Bible.

It's the Bible that needs to get opened from the outset – including in those groups organised for first-time enquirers. *The Bible should be opened in the very first session.*[1] No worries if someone is as yet unable to accept the authority and truth of the Bible; if we're in earnest to find out more, then we will be ready at the very least to look at the Scriptures, if only as interesting ancient documents. We don't even need to begin with a study on 'Why the Bible is the inspired Word of God.' Just let the pages speak for themselves and see what happens!

I remember meeting with some young people who had travelled to the famed 'Keswick Convention' in England's Lake District. "We've all become Christians, and go to various churches," they explained, "but no special groups have been organised for people like us, in our area. Have you got any advice for us?"

One way forward is simply to start a group yourself. With a video/dvd course it can be done *without any training*. "Just pop in the video", I once heard Billy Graham's daughter enthuse, "that's all you need." She was Anne Graham Lotz – herself internationally known as a Bible trainer of others. She was referring to some video TV Bible discussions (many of which she had shared in)

---

[1] One such course is *Christianity Explored* with Rico Tice, an international 10-week course with video/dvd and manual, following the life and claims of Jesus through Mark's Gospel. Enquiries: www.christianityexplored.com (0800 834 315).

and the study-guide that accompanied them. Ideal for student and church seminars, for home groups and also personal study, a phone call or e-mail enquiry is all that is necessary – to get hold of a cassette and simply start! These are used by many churches today. [2]

Eventually this is how even a nation becomes changed. One of the reasons why England was spared the revolutionary flames of neighbouring France in the late eighteenth century was that another kind of revolution had been under way ever since John Wesley's conversion to Christ in London, on Wednesday, May 24th 1738. It happened at a meeting for Bible study in Aldersgate Street, when John found his heart 'strangely warmed'. He and his brother Charles, who also found assurance of personal salvation, made their resolve *to change the course of history*. John Wesley became the greatest man of the century.

It was a Bible revolution that began to take hold of England. It was far from easy. Church after church, pulpit after pulpit were closed to the two preachers. The clods flew, and riots broke out in such places as Wednesbury, and St Ives. But everywhere that the Wesleys and their colleagues fanned out, little 'societies' were formed for the better understanding of the Scriptures. Today we call them fellowship groups, or home groups. Slowly, England became peace-loving. Towards the end of the century the

---

2 Among such group and personal Bible resources are the TV programmes *Open Home, Open Bible* – 60 video/dvd 15-minute studies (and study-guide) on the great Christian truths – and *Book by Book* – many video/dvd studies through whole books of the Bible (with study-guides); both products hosted by Paul Blackham and Richard Bewes. www.allsouls.org (020 7612 9773); for USA, www. visionvideo.com

local mayor would proclaim a public holiday when Wesley came to town.

Could it happen again? Of course it could, even though God does not seem to repeat his wonders in exactly the same form. The Scriptures never lose their power to change people, to change society, to change *you*. And it starts at the insignificant, the micro-level. It is utterly fascinating to read of the entry of the Christian faith into Europe for the very first time, around AD 49. It started with a little group of women at the riverside. 'We sat down,' records Luke, 'and spoke to the women who had gathered there' (Acts 16:13). No auditorium or stage, no riveting music, no powerful oratory even. Just a riverbank, and the apostle Paul, joined by Luke, Silas and Timothy. That was Europe's *Mission '49!*

A businesswoman, Lydia, was the first to respond to the message. The next thing was.... a house group! So we read in Acts 16:15. Move on a chapter, and a believer called Jason seems by then to have a house group organised (Acts 17:5,7,9). This was not popular with the authorities. In fact a riot takes place. Jason ends up in jail and the apostolic party has to move out of town. But that is how the European adventure began. Eventually the various religions that had been fused into a single towering world-view, dominating all of Europe, were to be replaced by the message of Jesus.

Today Europe is busily attempting to throw out its Christian culture, imagining meanwhile that it will still be able to hold together as a cultural entity. It is a false dream, and we must not be too surprised if we witness a reversion to what we have been before – a collection of squabbling heathen tribes. At the same time those churches that are committed to the steady teaching and sharing of the Scriptures will continue to expand.

"You will never be able to push back the secularist tide," dogmatise our critics. No? *But we are making the attempt.* It's been done before, however great the discouragements. They rioted when Paul was in Philippi. Back in Lystra he had been stoned. When he reached Athens they simply laughed. They might not have laughed so much if they could have known that the nearby temple of the Parthenon – looking as though it had been built only yesterday instead of 400 years earlier – would one day become a Christian church, and remain so for a thousand years.

The Christian outfit rarely looks like much! But to be part of a small group, gathered around the Scriptures – there is a potential in this very biblical pattern that can change a household, a street, a village.

Come to a field in Picardy, in France. It is the year 1520, June 4th, to be exact. There, England's most exotic king ever, Henry VIII, has set up a meeting with his French opposite number, Francis I. They are trying to establish a treaty of friendship, and for this they are putting on the most lavish spectacular that either of them has ever attempted. Beautiful draped pavilions, feasting, jousting, tournaments and flowing alcohol. It went down in posterity as 'The Field of the Cloth of Gold'. I remember doing it in history at school.

Can we match such a performance in the church? *Don't even think of trying.* For we are worshipping the King of Kings – the Son of Man himself. He is the glowing figure of Revelation's Rider on the White Horse; he's the heir of all creation. To think of dressing him up as Henry

VIII would be ludicrous – he doesn't need that! His glory is intrinsic to himself, and he tells us, "Where two or three come together in my name, *there am I with them*" (Matthew 18:20). A happening like that is for ever.

No lasting benefit resulted from the Field of the Cloth of Gold; its effects simply fizzled to nothing. Britain tried a slightly similar idea in London around Millennium time; we called it The Dome; children could have a happy time there, but as a nation-inspiring idea it failed, owing to the inadequate world-view that lay behind its creation.

It is the Incarnation – God coming among us in Christ – that adds the lustre and glory to every meeting of believing people around Jesus and his word. You can be in a little tin mission house in the back of nowhere, and there will be the glory of joint discovery; of getting to know the world's resurrected Saviour. Incarcerated in prison…. out in the scrub of the Sudan…. in the humblest home of Manhattan, *there can be glory*.

You can have your own Field of the Cloth of Gold in someone's bed-sit in New York or Birmingham; surrounded by a strange collection of Koreans, Greeks, Americans, Brits and Nigerians. And there, sipping a little coke or coffee, and sitting on a threadbare strip of carpet, you can meet – Bibles open, screen switched on – in Christ's name, and He, Master of the world, says, "*I'll join you.*" That is for ever. That is how lives are built. That is how even history gets changed.

5

GOING PUBLIC

From time to time I still have a nightmare, in which I am back at college all over again – and facing my final examination. Evidently the rules have been changed, and all those with qualifications have to obtain them again! Even in my dream I know that something is wrong: *I'm sure I shouldn't be here; it's ridiculous; I know I'm a London church minister; maybe I'll wake up in a minute.* But I don't seem to wake, and the moment of reckoning draws ever nearer.

Naturally, I'm unready; I've done no study, let alone revision – and the approaching deadline is on me.... and I'm caught out.

And then I do wake up! The sense of relief is indescribable. I lie there in the darkness, hugging the truth to myself; *it's all right; it all happened, way back. I passed!*

Now come to another nightmare – your own. There *you* are, a pathetic, unprepared individual, caught out. You're sitting in the examination chamber and you pick up the question paper; one look, and – *disaster*. Not one question can you even attempt. Your legs feel weak, and your tummy turns over with fright. At that point there's a tap on your shoulder. An anonymous official with specs murmurs in your ear,

"Excuse me, you shouldn't be here."

"Shouldn't be here?"

"That's right. You're not required to take this exam. You've already passed."

"*Passed?*" The room sways around you.

"Correct. Our records indicate that you don't need to take this exam. Look!" And a scroll of paper is waved before your eyes.

"*Your degree*," explains the patient official. "We don't want you here; you can go."

And dazedly you stumble out into the brilliant sunshine, clutching the piece of paper. You lie on the grass as the truth gradually sinks in. You've passed!

But this is only a pale reflection of the stunning good news released to our world in Christ.

To continue with the college scenario: If we students had been told that, by some miraculous twist of precognition, the results of the examinations *we had not yet taken* were now pinned up on the notice board for all to see, you can be sure that there would have been one concerted rush to look at the declared results.

When it comes to eternal issues, most of us would certainly be more than interested to know what the verdict of the end-time judgement on us was going to be – given that such a thing was possible. The Bible's good news is that it is not only possible; it is God's expressed desire that this should be so. Jesus himself expressed it as follows:

> *I solemnly assure you that the one who hears what I have to say and believes in the one who has sent me has eternal life.*

*He does not have to face judgement; he has already passed
from death into life (John 5:24 – Phillips translation).*

Already passed. The Gospel good news, then – what is
it? **It is the advance announcement, to believers, of the
future favourable verdict of the judgement upon them**.
Take it in, if you can. The moment you accepted that
Jesus Christ had borne your judgement for you upon the
cross – you passed from eternal death to eternal life. *Of
course* you are not going to face the judgement! Not for
your sins of the past, present or future. In unparalleled
love, God in Christ has already done it for you and he
is the guardian of your soul forever. Eternal life is yours,
here and now.

When this really dawns upon an individual, there's no
stopping them. A young Ugandan teacher, Festo Kivengere
accepted Christ, alone in his flat, one August Sunday
evening. "Give me one more week to live!" he exulted
in prayer. "Just one more week….and I'll tell everybody
in sight about this!" He rushed outside. A woman was
walking along the road 200 yards away. "Stop!" shouted
Festo. "I want to tell you! Jesus Christ has come my way
today!"

The woman tossed her head. She knew him of old,
drunk again!

By now some of his friends were coming out of evening
church. One look at Festo's face, and there was no need
for him to explain. They crowded into his quarters, and
stayed all night, celebrating, eating and talking. Then it
was Monday morning. Time for the Geography lesson.

"Sir, we don't understand. Your face… everything…
you're different!"

Festo had no option but to explain Sunday night.

"But…. how can we have what you've found? Can you tell us, sir?"

"So I told them," Festo confided to me one day in London. "Several of them became followers of Jesus then and there. This was the Geography lesson!"

Festo went on to become Director of Education for his region. Later he was to become an Anglican bishop, and co-founder of *African Enterprise*, which specialises in relief work and Christian witness in the great cities of Africa's continent. I was to become his UK Chairman. [1]

Witness….that was what the young teacher was doing from Day One of his beginning with Christ.

You can do that too. Maybe not to the extent of hijacking the geography lesson, but – in your own style – to give witness to what you know of Jesus Christ in your life. Often it is done by way of answering a question, as happened with Festo's pupils.

> *Always be prepared to give an answer to everyone who asks you to give the reason for the hope that you have. But do this with gentleness and respect…. (1 Peter 3:15).*

In a whole variety of ways we can show which side we are on; that we are disciples of Christ. At the beginning of the story Jesus had told his friends,

> *"You will receive power when the Holy Spirit comes on you, and you will be my witnesses in Jerusalem, and in all Judea and Samaria, and to the ends of the earth" (Acts 1:8).*

---

[1] *African Enterprise*: info@africanenterprise.co.uk, info@aeusa.org, aesa@africanenterprise.org.za, ae@africanenterprise.com.au

It means we are going public about our faith. But how is this best done, and how long am I to wait before I begin? Do I need some kind of special power pack first?

We witness for Christ immediately

Terrifying as it may sound, we can start at once. No, there is no need to wait for a power boost, as those apostles did, when their Master ascended from view. Then, certainly, they were required to wait for the coming of the Holy Spirit to empower the entire company of believers. This took place in Jerusalem within a few weeks. But from that time on, the gift of the Holy Spirit to every believer worldwide was always to be an essential part of the great Gospel offer. 'The forgiveness of your sins' *and* 'the gift of the Holy Spirit' were promised – from Peter's sermon at Pentecost onwards – to all who repented of their sins and turned to Jesus. The promise was given to 'all whom the Lord our God will call' (Acts 2:38,39). That holds for today!

The Scriptures teach that if we belong to Christ, his Spirit indwells us:

And if anyone does not have the Spirit of Christ, he does not belong to Christ (Romans 8:9).

The power of the Spirit of Christ is at work within us from the first moment of our response to him. We will take up this theme again in chapter 10; meanwhile accept that there is no reason why you should not be used as an effective 'witness' for Jesus Christ immediately!

We witness for Christ naturally

Speech, attitudes, friendships, work…. In a great variety of ways it will begin to emerge that there is a new dimension in the life of a Christian. It is not that Christianity is a new club, a new craze! It is, rather, that everything we touch and do will have a new enhancement about it.

And that applied even to the slaves, of whom there were sixty million in the Roman empire. Naturally there were believers among them. Critics have sometimes argued that the apostles ought to have urged Christian slaves to rise up against such an anti-Gospel system and throw off their shackles in revolutionary defiance of their masters. But to do that would have been to reduce Jesus to the level of a mere Spartacus, or Che Guevara.

In the event the members of the church did something more revolutionary still. Among themselves they treated the slave-master relationship *as though it didn't exist at all*; they simply ignored such demarcations. Meanwhile slaves were to render good service, and so 'make the teaching about God our Saviour attractive' (Titus 2:10). *The slaves of the Roman empire were to provide a working model of how to witness as a Christian*. The apostle Paul wrote to one believing slave-owner, Philemon, encouraging him to receive back his runaway slave (now a new Christian himself) 'no longer as a slave, but better than a slave, as a dear brother' (Philemon 15,16). In this and other instances a ticking time-bomb of Gospel principle was planted within the Roman empire. The day would come when Christian witness ensured that slavery was to be outlawed.

It is Christ who imparts this new quality to work, to wealth-creation, to our speech, our relationships, leisure, home and the family. The new life of a Christian, empowered by the Holy Spirit, will surface as an observable daily witness to our Lord – naturally! And people will notice.

We witness for Christ personally

There is a place for the public place 'soap-box' kind of Christian witness. I have done a little myself; standing on a chair or ladder in the full view of the public. Open-air work has its own effectiveness. The same is true with guest services in church, or the hiring of a hall for a sports dinner or arts evening. But nothing quite matches the one-to-one witness through personal friendship.

In the city of Brussels I remember being programme chairman of *Eurofest*. This was not, as might be supposed, the promotion of a new form of weed killer. *Eurofest* was a Bible event that attracted some 8,000 young people. It provided us, the organisers, with an ideal opportunity of establishing a profile of the average young European Christian. Accordingly we conducted a survey. Among the questions was this: *What was the chief influence behind your becoming a follower of Jesus Christ?* The boxes that could be ticked included, Family, Church Services, Media, Evangelistic Missions, and others.

When the results were released, the factor of lowest influence was *The Witness of a Stranger*. Far and away at the top, one box stood alone: *The Friendship of a Christian*.

That told us so much. Relationships count at every level. '**I had a friend**' – how often I have heard that! After all, Christianity itself is a relationship, and it was through one-on-one contacts that belief in Jesus spread like a bush fire in those early heady days of Christian witness.

Remember back to those words of Augustine! 'One loving spirit sets another on fire.' It is still true.

At some point you will be asked about your beliefs – on the university campus, within your own family, or by work colleagues, neighbours and close friends. *It cannot be avoided.* We should keep on the watch for natural opportunities of speaking about our faith; there is no need to force the issue, or to seem to be 'working round' to the subject of religion – people will soon learn to run a mile from what they perceive to be peddlers of an obsession.

Think it out; how you would say it….your reasons…. your discoveries. You are not there to pronounce on philosophical profundities. Frequently you will be unable to give a single answer to your critics – you are a beginner! But you will be like the man healed by Jesus; you will be able to say as a personal witness,

> *"One thing I do know. I was blind but now I see!" (John 9:25).*

We witness for Christ publicly

There are many ways of making a public affirmation of faith. I can think of some who stepped forward at the close of a great mission service, to register their decision in a public way. Christian believers are sometimes brave enough, a little later, to be interviewed about their story in a church service or at an outreach event; maybe to give in a short talk their 'testimony' to Christ. Take the opportunity if it is offered, but keep it short! What you were *before* coming to know him; *how* you came to be introduced to Jesus, and the difference that it is beginning to make now. It can sometimes help to preface the talk with a Scripture sentence that has come to mean much to you.

But there is one way of 'going public' that is endorsed in the Gospel itself, and should be common to every believer – and that is to *take your baptism seriously*.

Baptism….this is *the* outward distinguishing mark of the Christian. It signifies a farewell to the old life and an introduction to the new. It dramatises the inward washing from sin, achieved in the believer by the death of Jesus. It is also the *outward* counterpart and visual aid of the *inward* 'baptism of the Spirit' that initiates a new-born believer into the fellowship of Christians everywhere. Baptism is God's public mark on people who are his own. Jesus talked about it as he prepared his friends for his bodily departure:

> *"Therefore go and make disciples of all nations, baptising them in the name of the Father and of the Son and of the Holy Spirit" (Matthew 28:19).*

Christian baptism, instituted by Jesus, is one of the two great 'sacraments' of the Gospel (the Holy Communion being the other). It is a powerful outward symbol (water) of an inward and spiritual reality (cleansing from sin and the gift of the Spirit). It is always applied in the name of the Trinity, and it is something that every true church takes seriously.

"But," you may say. "I haven't been baptized."

This is something that can be talked over with the church leaders – they will have their own arrangements for Baptism and for the necessary instruction and preparation.

"Ah," you say, "but I was baptised as a baby."

This may mean that you are from an Anglican or Episcopalian background. If this is so, now that you are a believer, your church's interpretation should be that your baptism is now *completed*. The event itself – from beginning to end – points to the vital necessity of what the Gospel has made available, the washing away of our sins and the rebirth of our inner selves as new people.

Infant baptism, then, or 'believers' baptism? We do not have to quarrel between our different church traditions over the method of baptism, nor even over the amount of water used! In recent years Christians who take the Scriptures seriously in their teaching have learnt to refrain from attacking one another over Christ's wonderful ordinance of baptism. **Provided that inward personal faith has at some point completed the baptism, we may feel deeply honoured to be carrying this invisible mark of the Lord's possession of us.**

Some reading this page will have been baptised in infancy, and – having now come to faith – will be encouraged by their church leaders formally to underline and 'confirm' the promises that were made on their behalf at their baptism. A confirmation service is a public way of saying, "I am now a believer and a recognised church member in my own right, receiving the Holy Communion along with everybody else." The church, for its part, is confirming the fact. Even the Bishop turns up to mark the solemnity of such an event.

Other readers may have been 'dedicated' in infancy, and are now thinking carefully about being baptised. Whatever the pattern in the local church, the call is for Christians across the world to be bold and unashamed as they witness to a tottering, dying world, *and live up to their baptism.* It is a challenge to high standards!

Going public.... Is there anything apparent in our bearing, lifestyle and speech that makes people sit up a little and think? What are they hearing? Where does the difference lie? Is it noticeable that, like those Christian slaves in Rome, we are living models of a different way of living and a new kind of loving?

It was Sami Dagher, a church leader in the Middle East, who drew attention to the statement of a lawyer who had listened to a sermon on the way Christians are called to live and witness. The lawyer remarked,

> *"You know, if the Christians will live at this standard of Christianity, there will be no other religion in the Middle East!"*

Then let's emulate the very standard of Christ himself. He is the model for all time.

6

BECOME LIKE JESUS!

"Hey, could you stop the car?" I asked. "I can see a baobab tree and I have an urge to photograph it."

Bob Glen, a missionary friend from New Zealand, was driving me through Tanzania's scrubby terrain during an African visit. Obligingly he brought the Volkswagen to a halt and I dug out the camera.

I must have caught my fascination for baobabs from my father, in the early days of our life in East Africa. He was forever stopping by these incredibly thick and gnarled trees, gazing at them, measuring and photographing them. As a family of six, we would see if we could join hands around their massive trunks. Somehow, out in the arid African bush, the baobab is a symbol of enduring perseverance in a virtually rainless existence.

We who have begun with Jesus Christ can take a lesson from the many instances there are of survival and growth in alien environments. Add to the baobab tree of East Africa the edelweiss flower of the Swiss Alps as it clings to the inhospitable rocks that are its home…. and you may see a picture of yourself. There you are, holding bravely on, despite a surrounding world in revolt – scorched by conflicts and levelled down to a waterless plain by secularist advances and hostile world-views. And then you are urged as a believer to grow!

From the beginning of the church it has always been so. A further piece of imagery can bring encouragement at this point. Not the baobab tree so much as the Vine:

> *Abide in me and I in you. As the branch cannot bear fruit by itself, unless it abides in the vine, neither can you, unless you abide in me. I am the vine, you are the branches. Whoever abides in me and I in him, he it is that bears much fruit, for apart from me you can do nothing (John 15:4,5 ESV).*

Christ's words should give a lift to every believer who wishes to be *fruitful*. And 'fruit' is growth in Christian character. "By their fruit you will know them", said the Lord in his Sermon on the Mount. That was to be the eventual test of the difference between the true and the counterfeit believer. We will *expect* the genuine believer, with a true trust in Christ, to start producing the fruit of which the Sermon on the Mount speaks, in Matthew chapters 5-7 – namely, Christ-like characteristics!

It is not that we are *copying* Jesus, exactly. Nor is the 'fruit' to be added on to the believer, like decorations on a Christmas tree. Jesus chose his analogy carefully. He is the Vine, we are the branches; the power for Christ-like *living* is the natural result of our spiritual life in his, and his in ours. Union with Christ is the secret. "Abide in me and I in you." *Stay in touch!* Jesus is saying.

It is the unbreakable union with the Lord that accounts for the way in which Christian growth perseveres, even in the most unpromising circumstances. I'll never forget Ivan, from the borders of London, in Romford. Ivan wandered into the church I was then leading at St Peter's, Harold Wood, years ago.

"When's the dance beginning?" asked Ivan.

"Dance? There's no dance here; this is a Bible study. You can come to it if you like."

And with that, the young man, a nominal member of another belief-system, joined in the proceedings. Not that his Bible reading was up to much; in fact he couldn't read at all. Until a church member taught him to read we would see Ivan at worship, book upside-down, coping as cheerfully as he could. He became a Christian, and we watched the miracle of spiritual growth taking place in his life. Little by little the lifestyle that had periodically got him into trouble with the police began to alter. How hard it was! None of his friends or family had the slightest sympathy for his Christian decision. He got to know what it was to be thrown out, beaten up and disowned.

But Christ was at work in his life; we loved Ivan, and he loved us.

What causes a person to grow in this way? What principles operate? 'How,' a new Christian may be asking, 'can I make a success of this Christianity and become more like Jesus Christ?' The guidelines are simple enough:

Becoming like Christ is not sudden but progressive

Christian growth cannot happen overnight. No-one wakes up and declares, "How amazing – during the night I've become holy!" Certainly, the *start* can be an instantaneous occurrence; I have seen it many times. The moment we respond to Christ's message by repentance and faith – Click! – it is as instantaneous as the taking of a photograph. God accepts us into his family, forgiving us once and for all, and entering our lives by his Spirit. Freely!

They are justified by his grace as a gift, through the redemption which is in Christ Jesus (Romans 3:24 RSV).

Although we are still bad, God has declared us as just and righteous. We call this truth *Justification*. Think of yourself at the computer keyboard. As your typed words come up on the screen, you have an option as to whether you wish to 'justify' the crooked right hand margin of type, and so straighten it up to a fixed standard running perfectly down the page.

This is what God does for us spiritually. Although our record as moral beings is one of irreversible crookedness, God – by the power of Christ's saving death – not only forgives the repentant sinner. **He declares us to be lined up to match the very perfection of Christ himself.** We have been 'justified'. There is nothing like this truth in any other belief-system anywhere. It is unique to the Bible. Regardless of our sins, habits and all, at the cross we have been declared righteous and holy!

But of course we are not holy. Nevertheless, Justification is the start. To *progress* in character and to *become* holy in actual practice takes time. The Bible calls this process **Sanctification:**

For this is the will of God, your sanctification: that you abstain from unchastity (1 Thessalonians 4:3,4 RSV).

Learn the difference between justification and sanctification! Many Christians appear never to have sorted this out, and confusion results in their understanding. **Justification** happens initially, and in an instant. **Sanctification** happens gradually, progressively and sometimes painfully. When I was justified I was *declared* righteous. In the course of being sanctified, however, I am steadily being *made* righteous. 'Justification' is like the *click*, the initial snapping of the photograph on a traditional camera. 'Sanctification' is like the processing, the development of the film. It takes a lifetime!

Becoming like Christ is not a technique but a relationship

The process of growing as a Christian is not a technique. It is not like learning Swahili. It is a relationship. Becoming like Jesus in character and life can never be a matter of adopting the correct posture and ritual for worship or endlessly reciting the right number of prayers into the night. Jesus tells us that this is the way of the unbelieving heathen (Matthew 6:7). They think that they can be heard by the sheer repetition of their words. But Christ is no *guru*. And we are no mere devotees, learning a system. No; his words should warm the hearts of all who have come to love him:

I have called you friends (John 15:15).

Christianity on the personal level is a developing partnership, a daily adventure with a living Friend – *for life*. In this it resembles a marriage. But it would be a strange wedding if, at the end of the reception, the bridegroom were to say to his bride, "It's been a great day! Thank you ever so much for marrying me. The ceremony, the cake, the confetti – I loved every minute of it…. Well, see you around some time!"

God's great desire – in Christ – is to create a people for himself, *permanently and for ever*; godly, Christ-like men and women and whole families who, by their attitudes and choices, *remind* people everywhere of Jesus himself. And we ourselves are going to need perpetual reminders of the Christ that we walk with.

It is a walk of daily faith.

"We walk by faith, not by sight"(2 Corinthians 5:7).

The opposite of faith is *sight*; so this, then, is an invisible relationship. And yet ours is a reasonable faith – it is not a blind leap into the dark. We have been persuaded by the data available that God is real and alive; that he loves us in his Son, and that Christ – once crucified – is raised, ascended, and one day returning. But we are still not going to see him this side of the grave.

All that we shall receive from him by way of resources and spiritual strength will be *mediated* to us. We shall not see him, and there is no hotline word-of-mouth communication from him to us; no e-mails from heaven. But he is there, and he is with us, twenty-four hours round the clock.

This is where prayer, the Bible and Christian fellowship come into their own. And Christian discipline! It just will not all happen with me lying passively on my bed reading a magazine. Which leads us to a third guideline:

Becoming like Christ is not passive but active

This cannot be ignored. We are humans, not puppets. All the way along it is God who has generously taken the initiative on our behalf; revealing himself to us in Christ, speaking to us through the Bible's message and introducing us to the life of the church. *But we are invited to co-operate.* Victory over evil is promised to us – but are we willing to resist sin? It is not all one way. We can apply this to guidance as well.

God's guidance is available to us for the running of our lives. It comes partly through the great principles of the Scriptures – for God will never guide us to do something that is contrary to his revealed word. Guidance is also given through the promptings of the Holy Spirit in our prayers; it comes through the way in which our circumstances become shaped; it comes through the advice and shared wisdom of our Christian friends and leaders. *It does not, for the most part, get handed to us on a plate.* It is unlikely that we will be 'guided' as to where to take our next holiday. *Reason*: we are not puppets, nor are we animals. Our intelligence, our will and decision-making abilities are all called into play.

The promise of guidance is sure enough. "I will instruct you and teach you in the way you should go," runs the assurance of Psalm 32:8. "I will counsel you and watch over you." But read on!

> *Do not be like the horse or the mule, which have no understanding but must be controlled by bit and bridle (Psalm 32:9).*

We learn from this great principle that Christian growth and discipleship do not just happen, while we remain idle onlookers. Our own unique individuality is not going to be ironed out by God's leadership of our lives. Rather, energies and aptitudes will become enhanced and exercised as we engage with all that it means to be a Christian in a world that has lost touch with its creator.

Walk with Christ! we are urged in the New Testament. Wrestle! Work! Fight! Run! Resist! *These are all active terms.*

To grow in our life with Jesus can never be a do-nothing affair! No-one else will run our lives for us. Not for us the strange authoritarian churches and sects that would like to control and approve our every decision. We shall always be glad of the advice and leadership of more experienced Christians – but we are not disciples of *them*. We are disciples of one Man only. And yet, in the pursuit for holiness, the group around us will certainly have its part to play:

Becoming like Christ is not private but shared

Let's emphasise this again. Real Christianity can never be a solitary, private, esoteric week-end pursuit, a private course in self-improvement, assisted by Internet programmes, night school and tapes. In Jesus Christ we have been born into a family; an astounding assortment of badly matched personalities, eccentrics and misfits! *You are one of them.*

And the church is no mere club. All types, all accents, all nationalities crowd into the fellowship of Jesus Christ; yet we are on the same level around the Cross. A private religion? That's out. How terrifying! It is as Christ's new community that, together, we shall be called to give our service to an unfriendly world, to identify with its problems, to penetrate it with our own distinctive world-view, to battle with its prejudices and to take part in its debates. In doing so we shall undoubtedly get buffeted…. But this is part of the adventure – and of the growing process. Gifts and abilities will get stretched to the full in the service of our divine leader – and with a single joint aim….

> …. *Until we all reach unity in the faith and in the knowledge of the Son of God and become mature, attaining to the whole measure of the fullness of Christ. Then we will no longer be infants, tossed back and forth by the waves, and blown here and there by every wind of teaching….* *(Ephesians 4:13,14).*

It is a joint, a corporate goal. You are not on your own. Frequently we shall find that Christian growth is something that rubs off, from one to the other. We may find that we are not able to gain an accurate assessment of our own personal progress; others will be able to observe us better than we can ourselves. Our part is to focus – not upon ourselves, but upon Christ. There in him lies the standard of holiness, for us all.

Does it look like an unachievable goal? The atheist philosopher Bertrand Russell once commented on Christianity: "There is nothing to be said against it, except that it is too difficult for most of us to practise sincerely." What an understatement! It is not simply difficult; without the indwelling power of the Holy Spirit it would be *impossible*. This theme we must take up in a future chapter. But, for the present, let us face the question, Why did we ever start?

Let John Newton, author of the hymn *Amazing Grace* state the position. A blaspheming slave trader in earlier life, he became – after his conversion to Christ – an outstanding evangelist and Anglican vicar. He once said, *"I am not what I ought to be; I am not what I wish to be; I am not what I hope to be; but, by the grace of God, I am not what I was!"*

Take a second look at those words of a Christian's growing experience. They will find a welcome echo in every struggling – yet growing – believer.

7

SURPRISED BY SUNDAY

It was Sunday that gave me my love of avocado pears. We actually grew them at the first home that I can really remember, on the lower slopes of Mount Kenya. Many were the times that we started off a new tree! With some difficulty you insert a matchstick right through the hard kernel of an avocado; the shiny brown thing is then suspended over a vase – half in and half out of the water.

That is just the start. Even at the age of five I found myself wondering how wild avocados could ever have managed without vases and matchsticks. But I did know that – done our way – a tree would eventually result, producing fruit in seven years' time. It is not surprising that I was not to taste any product from 'my' trees until many years later when I revisited our old home. Amazingly the trees had matured.

Being in somewhat short supply, avocados tended to be a Sunday speciality – as were other features of our urban-free existence. Sunday was not a day for work, maintained my missionary parents. But certain 'occupations' were brought out on Sunday only, and I looked forward to them. We created a *papier mâché* model of our neighbourhood. On it we simulated the dusty red road that led to our house, the nearby wattle trees and Australian blue gums, the church built by Dad and the house lived in by neighbouring missionary 'Auntie Lorna'. Sunday was also my introduction to the world of painting, paper chains and printing – as I experimented with potato cuts for the first time.

Naturally we did church too, although – our area having become caught up in the great Revival of East Africa – the services were so packed and of such length, that we children would only stay in for a proportion of the proceedings, before being taken back home. However we grew up bi-lingual. I can still sing *Blessed Assurance* in Kikuyu.

There were no western-style shops, no gas, no electricity, no running water (and therefore no taps in the bathroom), no telephone, no postal service, no sanitation and no doctor for twenty miles. Our clothes were largely home-made, Mum gave us school lessons on weekdays and our entertainments were self-devised. *Sunday was our highlight.* Special food, special activities, tea with Auntie Lorna – with her famous flourless, butterless, eggless, sugarless cake…. and Dad would be at home.

'One day in seven'; the Creator actually *designed* this to be the week's highlight – not simply for his worshipping people, but for the inhabitants of the whole world. For the principle goes back to the very beginning of things:

> *By the seventh day God had finished the work he had been doing; so on the seventh day he rested from all his work. And God blessed the seventh day and made it holy, because on it he rested from all the work of creating that he had done. (Genesis 2:2,3)*

Before that first call to Abraham – and longer still before the giving of the Ten Commandments – the principle of the seventh day was stamped indelibly into nature's complex mechanism and the life of the human race. Here is what Bible students call a *creation ordinance*.

Another creation ordinance – later endorsed by Jesus – was the divine blue-print of the one man/one woman marriage partnership (Genesis 2:24). That, too, goes back to the beginning of our civilisation. Tamper with either of these creation laws, and our life here begins to fall apart in bewilderment and discontent – even though society itself may not know why it is dissatisfied.

We can illustrate this from the attempt to abolish the traditional week at the time of the French Revolution over 200 years ago. The task of drawing up a new republican calendar was entrusted to Charles Gilbert Romme, assisted by a group of able mathematicians. From September 1792, the year was to be divided into twelve months of thirty days each, every month being divided into three periods of ten days. These were called decades, the last day of each of these new 'weeks' being a day of rest.

What happened? It didn't work. The scheme was officially abandoned on January 1st, 1806. *Lesson*: Don't fool around with creation ordinances!

Far from being a constraining burden on men and women, the one day in seven should be understood as a delight. To many who embark upon the Christian life, Sunday comes as an unexpected and joyful surprise. Once a believer can see it as a day freed up once more by Christ, it becomes what it was always intended to be, a one-in-seven heaven-provided gift. As the nineteenth century Scottish minister Thomas Chalmers put it: *We need scarcely speak on the details of Sabbath observation to him who already loves that hallowed day.*

Look forward, then, to Sunday! Despite the fact that in some parts of the world Sunday is officially a work day (in which case the churches have adapted their programme accordingly), Sunday has come to be recognised generally as the day set aside for rest and worship by at least two billion people. Certain Christian traditions choose to retain the traditional Jewish Saturday as their Sabbath day…. but the creation ordinance as a principle is practically universal for our entire human race. *One day in seven is special.*

It's Creator's Day

Here are the words again. "And God blessed the seventh day and made it holy." It could be argued that this truth was hardly news to Christ's Jewish listeners, when he taught about it on the shores of Lake Galilee. *Yet they had a problem.* The sheer power and emphasis of that seventh day had been hijacked by the human traditions of the religious leaders at that time – the Pharisees. They had effectively killed the Sabbath day, subjecting it to a straitjacket of stern traditions and detailed rules, that made it virtually impossible to observe. Instead of being the Creator's day, it had become *their* day, and a day of oppression at that.

In declaring that the Sabbath was made for man and not man for the Sabbath (Mark 2:27), Jesus was re-establishing the Sabbath as a universal day of respite, modelled upon the Creator's own example – and not merely for Israel, but for all humanity.

It's Liberation Day

The one-in-seven day was intended to be like an island of refreshment after a week of energetic output; a precious few hours, setting men and women and whole families free – to take a break, and restore spiritual vision. The Pharisees for their part had done everything *but* set people free! Jesus put the picture very clearly:

> *They tie up heavy loads and put them on men's shoulders, but they themselves are not willing to lift a finger to move them (Matthew 23:4).*

The Pharisees' view was that if you were very careful and walked very slowly, and took innumerable precautions on the day before, you might just squeeze through the Sabbath without sinning. However, Jesus – the greatest burden-bearer the world has ever known – lifted the seventh day, freed it from its shackles, and made it a day of liberation.

Naturally it was to be a day of liberation for workers. A good idea? A day to be protected? A nationally agreed bank holiday once a week, when – as far as possible – the machinery is switched off and the shutters go up? It was very welcome to me at the age of eighteen!

It was then that I spent my gap year working in Peek Frean's biscuit factory in London's Jamaica Road. I was managing a machine in the Sugar Plant; working overtime in a dim, twilight world of whirling flour and sugar dust and getting up at 4.30 in the morning to clock in on time. Talk of liberation – how we looked forward to the week-end!

But this divine institution is also a day of liberation for the needy. Jesus, by his concern, and indeed because of miracles performed on the Sabbath, gave the day something it had never quite had before. It was said by

John Chrysostom at the turn of the fourth century that the Jewish Sabbath, rather than being 'dissolved' by the Christian Sunday, had been 'enhanced' by it. He was referring to the mercy and service aspect that Jesus had given to the day.

From this, Christian people have learnt to make Sunday a hospital visiting day, a 'Teach the Children' day, a day for inviting in college students and internationals living far from home. Sunday, when treated like this, can shine in the week like a beacon of fellowship for many who look for a touch of Christ and his love. Further, by the message of the singing and the preaching, Sunday by Sunday, men and women across the centuries have been set free from their sins and their burdens – by the million! It is happening every week.

It's Resurrection Day

No special command was given, no enactment enforced…. yet, little by little, the old Jewish Sabbath came to be displaced by the Christian Sunday. *Saturday or Sunday?* There should be no heavy controversy about this. Both are in line with the Scriptures. The commandment reads, 'Six days you shall labour and do all your work, but the seventh is a Sabbath to the LORD your God' (Exodus 20:9,10). The principle is clear: It is not the seventh day *of the week* that is defined as holy, but the seventh day after *six days of labour*.

This may comfort some who, because of pressures brought to bear upon them find themselves unable to observe the accepted Christian Sunday and must therefore find some form of mid-week Sabbath-keeping alternative. There are churches, indeed, that have created more than one new mid-week service for this very purpose.

We should note, however, that the dramatic change to Sunday after centuries of established tradition, is one strong pointer to the proof of the bodily resurrection of Jesus Christ. If his resurrection had only been a beautiful piece of wishful thinking, the legend might have persisted for a generation, only to be flattened out by the tide of history like a child's sandcastle on the beach. And without question the Sabbath would have remained unchanged.

Only an event that demonstrably altered our view of the universe could possibly have brought about such a switch. For when does the church commemorate Christ's resurrection? At Easter? No, we are doing it every Sunday! The first Christians really believed that Christ's tomb was empty on that first day of the week; that the apostles had seen the Lord; that Jesus was the powerful winner over death and darkness; that all authority in heaven and on earth belonged to him. Every Sunday that the Christian church met together represented a challenge to the claim of the Roman Caesar to his title of *Dominus et Deus* ('Lord and God').

We must emphasise it again; no command was given for the change-over to Sunday. *There was no need*, such was the explosion of joy at the ending of death's night. Even in New Testament times there were hints of this change in Sabbath observance. Paul and the Christians of Troas met on the first day of the week 'to break bread' (Acts 20:7). The apostle instructed his converts to have their money gifts ready 'on the first day of every week' (1 Corinthians 16:2).

At first, Jewish believers in Christ had continued to meet as usual in their synagogues – until they were forced out. Then it became common for them to meet together for worship on Saturday evenings. Under the first century

Roman emperor Trajan these evening worship occasions evidently became illegal. In a very natural transition, then, Christian worship moved to a Sunday – and that final development cut the last links with the old Sabbath, and gave the Christian rest day its resurrection dimension.

One of the biggest changes in a new Christian involves our view of Sunday. It begins to dawn upon us that it can be wonderfully different from another workday, or a day spent in trudging round shops. You may not have an Auntie Lorna to go and have tea with, but *Sunday* – why, it's a whole seventh of your life! See if you can put a little creative thought into it. And work out an *arrangement*, by which you will focus that day of rest on your Creator, on your resurrected Lord, and the worldwide family – your family – that has been so marvellously created by the fellowship of the Holy Spirit.

8

AT CENTRE-POINT –
THE CHURCH!

A pagan philosopher of Rome, Celsus by name, was writing with quivering pen around the year AD 178. He was singling out the Christian church for his bitterest, most jeering criticisms. How did he interpret the church's mission? Celsus worded it as follows:

> Let no man come to us who is learned or wise or prudent; but whoso is stupid or ignorant or babyish, he may come with confidence. The only converts we care to have (or indeed can get) are the silly, the ignoble and the senseless; the slaves, the women and the children. [1]

By such phrases Celsus was describing what he viewed as the most contemptible and pathetic categories of society. The terms used by modern critics will be very different, but today we are just as likely as ever to find ourselves on the receiving end of disparaging and insulting epithets thrown at Christ's mission. "If they persecuted me," said

---

1 *True Discourse, c 178 AD*; see 'Early Church History to AD 313, HM Gwatkin, MacMillan 1909, p.174.

Jesus, "they will persecute you also" (John 15:20). How feeble and ineffective we are made to look! You would think that Christianity was the world's most shrinking body of belief rather than its biggest.

Why bother to be a Christian in the first place? Certainly not because discipleship is particularly comfortable! In the last analysis the big reason *for becoming a Christian is that Christianity is true*. We should be glad to know the truth for the truth's sake; the truth about ourselves, about the universe and its purpose, what life is for and where everything is heading.

Is our mission statement as gutless as Celsus tries to make it? Not according to God, declared the apostle Paul. The church is integral to God's all-time plan....

> ....*which he purposed in Christ, to be put into effect when the times will have reached their fulfilment – to bring all things in heaven and earth together under one head, even Christ (Ephesians 1:9,10).*

If you were to read such words from the Manifesto of any movement, secular or religious, you would wonder whether its initiators were pursuing an impossible aim – a goal that puts the plans of Alexander the Great or Ghengis Khan into the shade, for its sheer unattainability!

To bring all things? In heaven and on earth? *Together?* Under the banner and rule of a single overall head, Jesus Christ? The historian, T.R. Glover, has written of the early church:

> *The task was enormous. No one, I think, can even begin to measure it who has not stood alone in the swarming*

*population of some great city in a heathen land. Then he
will understand the incredulity and contempt with which
a Celsus can contemplate the Christian dream of bringing
all the races with all their differing traditions, faiths,
philosophies and cultures under the single law of Christ.[2]*

But this is what the New Testament brazenly sets
out as the church's programme; that everything is to be
brought together in Christ. *Basic* to the plan's fulfilment
is the church itself. Its members were to model this to
the world. "We'll begin with you Ephesians!" was Paul's
message. Is it *uniformity* that God is after? No; the church
is an amazing cake-mix of personalities and backgrounds.
Is it *unanimity*, then? N-n-no! It is enough that Christians
take the Scriptures as their authority, accept Jesus as Lord
and Saviour, and baptise in the Name of the Trinity. When
this happens, you have a church – even if you do not have
perfect agreement on forms of church government, dress
codes, musical tastes or the running of church services.

What the Lord of the church desires is *unity*; unity in
himself and in the apostolic Gospel – unity, along with
diversity! I sensed this as strongly as I had ever felt it before,
at a great congress for evangelistic preachers, organised in
August 2000 by Billy Graham. We numbered over 11,000
delegates and were drawn from 211 countries. It was the
most internationally representative gathering, secular
or religious, in all history, eclipsing even the Olympic
Games and the United Nations. Some of those attending
had come out of the forests, some from mountain and
desert areas. One man had walked 400 miles to attend

2 *The Influence of Christ in the Ancient World*, CUP 1933, p. 78.

the congress. One woman had paddled her way up the Amazon to reach the nearest airport. We were drawn from an amazing kaleidoscope of different Christian traditions and denominations.

Yet from beginning to end of those electric eight days we were completely one. There was no divisiveness, no controversy; we were gathered as one body around the Bible and its message of the Lord. At the closing Communion I found myself hugged by Africans, kissed by bearded Argentinians and holding hands with Koreans. Some atheistic guards from a totalitarian regime had come. They were there to keep a stern watch on the delegates from their own country – yet several of them came to faith in Christ during that moving Communion service. I remember thinking to myself, *With such powerful recognition of one another as sisters and brothers in Christ's great church, what can ever stop us?*

'The Church.' The term comes from the Greek New Testament word *ecclesia*; it simply means those who have been 'called out'. Described a hundred years ago by the Methodist scholar George Findlay as the 'Society for the abolition of Sin and Death', the church's role is central to what God is doing in the world. *To no other body of people has the Son of God pledged his presence.* Get any group of believers together, big or small, and we can be sure that Christ is there among them.

And we have been 'called out' as God's strategic task force, to inflict as much damage as we can on the kingdom of darkness!

That is not how we are always pictured. Years ago I was once dressed as King for a staff pantomime that we were putting on at All Souls Church. We were doing

Aladdin. In my office I was carefully adorning myself with flowing drapes and false beard, with ornaments and tinsel – topping everything off with the office teapot cover on my head.

Stepping into the outer office, I was suddenly confronted by a stranger. He was one of the homeless of London's streets. Somehow he had found his way to the inner recesses of our church. He was looking for a blanket for the night. For a long second he stared at me, unwinkingly, taking everything in. Then he spoke.

"You the vicar?"

That was his immediate assumption. To him, I – dressed like a Christmas tree – was obviously the vicar! I felt completely wrong-footed.

"Er, I'm *one* of the vicars," I muttered, by way of reply. It was all I could admit to! Pointing him to where he could obtain the required help, I then went out to join the cast, feeling pathetic and demoralised. It was only hours later that I began to giggle at the absurdity of it all.

The robes, droning voices, antiquated terminology, dust-laden books and the smell of bats…. it is taking us a while to redress the caricature – often self-inflicted – that in many quarters has built up around the image of the church. Be thankful if you have been introduced to a con-gregation where the style of operation is under continu-ing and prayerful review. We will never get it completely right, but if prayer and the Bible are prominent in the life of the church, then the overwhelming impression to new-comers will be one of warmth and reality, simply because *Christ* is in it all.

Important? Unbelievably so. It is up to us, who have been 'called out', to make Jesus – the most perfect being who ever walked on earth – visible to as many people as possible. More – we are to be his 'fulness' to every generation:

> *And God placed all things under his feet and appointed him to be head over everything for the church, which is his body, the fulness of him who fills everything in every way (Ephesians 1:22,23).*

True, if someone takes the trouble to read the Gospel stories, they can obtain a perfect portrait of Jesus, but they still need to 'see' him in flesh and blood terms.

The picture needs filling out. That's our cue, and it was the cue for those Ephesian Christians to whom the apostle Paul was writing. Some of those citizens of that 1,000-year-old city must have gulped when they read of the plan involving the church of Jesus Christ. They would have strolled along the seventy foot boulevard running up from the harbour to the great theatre of Ephesus. They would have glanced up at the all-dominating Temple of Artemis – four times the size of Athens' Parthenon. It was depicted on Roman coins; it was one of the seven wonders of the world. They would have gazed around at the city's teeming population of 300,000 and wondered in awe how such a towering pagan belief-system could ever be challenged by a world-view championed by an apostle chained in prison.

But it was going to happen. Those ninth and tenth verses of Ephesians chapter one form the key to the whole letter. *Christ* – who was to be proclaimed to the world – will bring all things in heaven and on earth together, under himself.

For he is the single, unifying reason why we call this system around us a universe, not a 'multiverse'. The whole thing holds together in him. I remember former London colleagues, Tom Parsons and Stephen Nichols, explaining to the students at All Souls Church about the very origin of 'universities'. The very word comes from two Latin words, *uni* ('one') and *veritas* ('truth')....*one truth*. It was Christians who said, "Let's start universities!" They founded these places of learning in order to study the truth, the one truth that was viewed as a single, coherent story. Every subject – whether physics, music or mathematics – was a separate chapter in a single over-arching story; different slices, but all from one cake. Colleges were founded, and as often as not they were given biblical names. In the university of Cambridge we had Jesus College, Trinity College, Christ's College, St John's College. My own college was Emmanuel.

Across the West over the last 300 years, a significant loss of confidence has come to result in today's wide collection of highly diverse and irreconcilable stories. There are now as many 'narratives' as there are narrators; there is 'my' story, 'your' story, the Marxist story, the feminist story. "You can now branch out," declared Tom and Stephen, "into Star Trek and David Beckham studies!" The result is a generation of students in the West – not to mention politicians – who, more than any other in living memory, are unable to give a credible account of the meaning of life. Today, in many quarters, the idea that there is one story, one factor, one Person that interprets and makes sense of all life tends to be dismissed; meanwhile the Barbarians now largely occupy the seats of power in the media, as well as in great areas of government.

This is not going to stop the onward march of Christ's church. For some centuries we have been a somewhat protected church in the West; now we are out in the open again, exposed to the barbs of anti-Christian powers – and we shall certainly be the stronger for it. Already we are learning from our African, Asian and South American friends who have rarely enjoyed much protection, and are showing us how the church operates and thrives when it is under pressure. The growth rate of some of these churches is sensational.

While we will never be in the majority, we are targeting the whole world with the love of Christ! In our local churches we are to practise the uniting principle of Ephesians 1:9,10 with confident expectation. There will be laughing Celsus figures who will maintain that we can never win the world. No? *But we are making the attempt.* Could one turn London, Buenos Aires, Lagos, Kansas City into a church? Um....Let's try! If Christ came for everybody, then no one is exempted from the loving witness of his people:

> *But you are a chosen people, a royal priesthood, a holy nation, a people belonging to God, that you may declare the praises of him who called you out of darkness into his wonderful light (1 Peter 2:9).*

The vital lesson of history is not to embark on this exercise alone. Do that, and you will be wandering around some great city, dropping in at one centre, tasting worship at another, drifting from fellowship to fellowship – and always in a spiritual muddle; you will eventually be picked off by one or other of the enemies of the Gospel.

We need that steady, constant circle of recognised fellow-worshippers who will miss us if we are away from them for more than two weeks.

After all, Jesus came, not to found a new philosophy, but a new *Community*, and if we belong to him, then we belong to a local manifestation of his church. The church is described in the New Testament as a **Body**, with Christ as its Head; as a **Bride**, with Christ as the Bridegroom; as a **Building**, with Christ as the Foundation. From these images we are to understand the church's vital relationship of dependence upon Jesus himself; our very existence as a people derives from him.

Which church? Pray about it. Draw up your own checklist. Is it a church where they take the Scriptures seriously? Is the Bible opened and used in public exposition? How much does prayer feature there? Does it have a rounded Gospel and Bible approach to life, people and families – or is it only a single-issue church, with some special 'thing' or unusual doctrine that characterises it? Could you, with reasonable confidence, introduce a friend to it without being embarrassed? What emphasis is placed there upon the Cross? Do they hold periodic services of Holy Communion, besides the regular worship services? Are the arrows of concern, evangelism and service pointing in a healthy direction outwards into the surrounding community, or is the church only focused internally upon its own affairs?

A warning: you will never, ever find a perfect church. However, should you be successful in finding one, it would be wise not to join it – **because it would immediately cease to be perfect.**

9

THE FOUR PLANKS

"Would you like to describe to us your world-view?" I was in the chair and there were five or six of us members of the Board of Governors, interviewing candidates for the post of Head Teacher at a London school. The short list was down to three candidates, and we were having them in, one after another, for interview. It is a useful question to put during an interview for any post. The question to be asked is not "Have you got a world-view?" – because every man, woman and child on earth does possess a certain viewpoint! The question – in the form we put it to each candidate in turn – was designed to reveal *the depth and credibility* of their basic understanding about all existence. It was the final question, and it drew out a virtually identical response every time:

"Would you like to describe to us your world-view?"

"Oh!.... um, *world-view?*"

"Yes. All we mean by that is your personal interpretation of the meaning of life on this world."

"Oh!....er, well, I think I would need a bit of *time* to be able to go into that!"

"No, no; bullet points will be fine."

All three candidates fell flat on their faces at that last

hoop. They were stumbling, scrabbling desperately for a form of words that would make some sense to our interviewing board.

I summed things up with my colleagues later, "We all know that education is far more than learning to add up figures correctly and getting your spelling right. The whole point of education is to help boys and girls establish their relationship to the universe! And if," I added, "these aspiring head teachers haven't got that sorted out for *themselves* yet, why on earth should we appoint them?"

It didn't take us long to decide; we felt unable to make an appointment, and readvertised.

"Go on then," I once challenged a critic at a party, "give us your alternative to Christianity, your *own* world-view. What do you believe?"

"Well," came the reply, "I'm an atheist."

"Oh, come," I said; "I'm not asking you what you *don't* believe. I'm asking what you *do* believe about life on this world."

It was then that my friend began to flounder and sound unsure of himself. That he had a world-view I would not dispute. But his seemed to be a very inadequate framework for life; one, I suggested, that would ultimately give way under pressure, and let him down.

There is no case for Christian believers to be smug or cocksure in their understanding of the world around them. There is plenty to challenge and embarrass us in the views we hold. The scandal of church divisions and factions, to take one example. The problem of evil and of human suffering, to take another. Yet we would firmly maintain that, while there are problems that call for heartsearching and painstaking study, our perplexities are nothing compared with those that confront our unbelieving friends! For they are having to try and make sense of birth and life, of calamities and eternity, from an intellectual basis that is constantly shifting on a sea of relativities. Quite often their views are formed by thinkers whose books will have ended up in second-hand charity shops within a decade or two.

The Christian has been bequeathed a framework of given biblical revelation that has withstood many centuries of rigorous criticism. Certainly there are difficulties that tax us to the limit, but these difficulties are themselves accommodated within the world-view that is ours. *They are actually built into it.* The problem of evil? For many thinking people it is an unsolvable mystery. As for us, we wrestle with it – but the Scriptures have already taken it into account and have given us a framework to work with.

If we simply take the question 'Who are we?' it needs to be recognised that this is scarcely being asked at all around the West. 'What are we here for? What lies behind life as we see it around us? What is the whole thing about?' These are blockbusting issues, but such is the blinding power of material ambition and short-term goals that they tend only to surface in the face of financial ruin, family breakdown or health crises.

Don't wait for the crisis, should be the message to our friends. The fact that a man or woman has not worked out a rationale for being a citizen of Earth is itself a crisis! I recall seeing one of Britain's top politicians being interviewed years ago by Michael Parkinson on BBC Television. It was a scintillating performance. Then came the closing question:

"And as you enter the twilight, so to speak, of your

long career, how do you view the future, even your own demise and departure from this world?" I had never heard Parkinson ask such a question before. Nor since. The reply was an eye-opener.

"Oh…. my death, you mean? Er, yes, well…. I mean…. I dare say I'll face that when the time comes. I'll, er….well, I'll hope that I can probably muddle my way through in the end."

As I switched off the programme, I thought, *That man, with all his cleverness, has not given ten minutes' thought to the question of his own death and what lies beyond. His understanding of the future seems to be a blank.*

Back to us, then, and our worked-out view. For by now we ought to know that we are more than blobs of protoplasm wrapped around an appetite.

My own world-view is constructed as a raft. Beneath me are the heaving seas of the most unstable era in history. All around are the rocks and currents of modern thought. But my plan is clear. If I can build my raft securely enough, formed with planks of enduring strength *and Bible truth*, then I can have every hope of negotiating the many hazards around me and emerge through the whirling spray, intact and riding high.

Such a raft takes time to build. Many believers possess only a random collection of pet Scripture verses, and some Bible stories. When put under the spotlight they have nothing to say on major issues confronting the modern world. Yet of all people, we are the ones with the answers to today's dilemmas! This is because right at hand is the Book which has steered and equipped God's people across the centuries – through wars, the rise and fall of mighty movements, and revolutions too many to count.

It will do the same thing again for us in our own generation.

I was once about to engage in a debate with members of another religion. I decided beforehand to read their authorised holy book.

"What did you think of it?" someone asked, when I had finished.

"I can only say – having read it – that I just love the Bible!" was my reply.

A biblical world-view. What is central to my raft? That's easy. We start with Christ – God's self-revelation for all time, universally. We have touched on this in the previous chapter.

Sometimes people are heard to say, "I can't see where Jesus fits in!" They do well to learn from one of Christianity's greatest students, Athanasius of the fourth century, Egyptian-born and Greek-educated. He declared, *The only system of thought into which Jesus Christ will fit is the one in which he is the starting point.*

If we lose that understanding, the whole thing will be a muddle. We will be like the man, who buttoned up his shirt, beginning with the wrong button. He could say, "Oh well, I'll keep on trying; maybe it will work out in the end".... but it won't!

We start with Christ. He must be like the flag at the top of the mast in the very centre of my raft. I ought to be able to say to the people who question me, "Mine is essentially a Christian world-view – with Jesus Christ at the centre."

He is before all things, and in him all things hold together (Colossians 1:17).

Jesus did not begin half-way through history. He is part of the eternal Godhead. Way back in the Old Testament we can observe that numbers of times in its recorded events he is seen to be at work as the pre-incarnate Second Person of the Trinity.

Sometimes he is recognised as 'the sent one' – 'the angel of the Lord' (as contrasted with '*an* angel of the Lord') – leading his people and indeed speaking as God himself, with divine attributes. You have only to read Genesis 22:11,12, Exodus 3:2-6 or Judges 2:1, and plenty of similar passages, for this to become apparent. Christ is the interpreter of all history; he is presented as the only candidate from the entire human race who can break open the seals of the scroll that contains the meaning of life. By his coming and by his saving death upon the Cross, he makes sense of our existence – and heaven itself rejoices:

> *And they sang a new song: "You are worthy to take the scroll and to open its seals, because you were slain, and with your blood you purchased men for God from every tribe and nation" (Revelation 5:9).*

Centred upon Christ, then, my raft will need to be formed of some durable planks that will support me as I cling tight to the testimony of Christ who holds all things together. What are these planks? Why, they are the mighty truths running through Scripture; they are basic to our entire belief-structure. There are four of them. John Stott has described them as 'epochs' or 'events'.

The plank of Creation

This is not a matter of a few proof texts. It runs throughout

Scripture, and from it we learn that we are not simply a collection of biochemical reactions within an impersonal and haphazard mechanistic universe. The universe holds no terrors for us. We are God-like beings, amazingly the summit of the Creator's activity, formed in his image and designed for fellowship with himself. This world, with its teeming life, is no chance event. It is our home, and we have been made its custodians.

The Methodist leader, Dr Donald English, was speaking once of his excitement at this discovery, as a new Christian. "There's an old Gospel song", he said, "which has as its refrain, *I can't feel at home in this world any more*. Of course I know what that is supposed to mean, but my claim is that I do feel at home in this world – at last!"

The plank of the Fall

Once take in the fact of our human fall into rebellion, and so much fits into place! God-like beings we were indeed created, and still are to this day – but we are flawed. The choice facing Adam and Eve was not between good and evil, for as innocent beings they had no knowledge of evil. The choice was between going with the Lord God or taking their own independent course. Goodness was not programmed into them; they were not puppets or automata. They were people with wills, and they could choose.

And because they were prototype, *representative* man and woman, when they fell, they took the human race with them into judgement. This fact runs through Scripture, and it lies behind all sin, evil, suffering and human conflict.

Traditional Marxists never believed in any concept of a Fall. They believed in a kind of utopian ideal, a workers' paradise, achievable in this life – the only life that they acknowledged. They were always doomed to disillusionment, and it was inevitable that across great tracts of the thinking world their belief-system was going to let them down.

Thoughtful Christians will grieve and weep over the evil things that take place in our world, but we are not actually surprised at them. This whole scenario of the Fall is built into our thinking as Bible people, and we take account of it realistically, in all our service and witness to a dying world. The Fall is a vital plank in our world-view. *It explains so much.*

The plank of Redemption

Here is our point of godly optimism. God has done everything necessary, in and through Christ, to reclaim us for himself. Here is a world in defiance of its Creator – but even at the point of our departure from fellowship with God, the process was beginning by which our banishment from the divine presence was to be met by suffering love, and finally reversed.

The Cross stands astride the whole story of the Bible. The theme of sacrifice for sin is woven deep into the story of God's dealings with his ancient people the Jews, from their earliest beginnings. They would never forget the sacrifice of the Passover lamb at the time of their rescue from Egypt; nor the sacrificial system in the Tent of Worship of which we read in the books of Exodus and Leviticus. The training went deep into the life of all Israel; one day there would be the one and only Sacrificial Lamb for the sins of the world for all time – how could there ever be another?

When you come to Christ who has died for your sins – and begin to live for him in the power of his momentous resurrection – you will go back in your mind and spirit to the Cross again and again. You will be like those Brazilian citizens who, every day for a full year, were treated to the spectacle on their televisions of an amazing goal scored by the footballer Pele – there were no complaints! *For you, the Cross – and its fantastic sequel of the Resurrection – will colour the whole of your mindset.* The universal breadth of Christ's redemption means that every person and situation is redeemable! This affects your witness, your plans, your prayers. You will never give up on anybody. And you will know yourself to be a debtor to the love of Christ every day. Why, the Cross will have become your way of life.

The plank of the final triumph

The future scene. Yes, we've only to read the last page of the Bible, and we see the Garden of Eden restored – now as a garden *city*. The final Judgement has taken place; evil has been dismantled in smoking ruins, the tree of life is offering its fruit to the nations, the Fall has been reversed, resurrected glory is ours and redemption is complete, goodness is the undisputed winner and the returning Christ has ushered in his kingdom of truth and love for ever. The Bible – which took fifteen hundred years to write – has this astonishing consistency; so that the beginning exactly matches the ending, with Genesis finally shaking hands with Revelation.....*and the story is complete.*

Ask many modern people for their views about the future, and they will tend to come up with doomwatch predictions, apathetic speculation, or just random guesses. Not so the biblical believer. Christ is coming back, suddenly, publicly and universally. The universe will itself be rejuvenated and restored as the new heaven and new earth take over, and the church, as a bride, is caught up with Christ its Bridegroom, to be with him in unimaginable glory.

Four planks, making up a raft, centred in Jesus Christ. If I can build my world-view upon this raft, I shall find that I can ever-increasingly ride this world's turbulences, win its arguments and make sense of its dilemmas. Wealth-creation? Why, the planks of Creation, the Fall and Redemption all relate to this one issue; *we will have something to say*. Racism? We can speak from all four planks on this. Politics? Try the Fall and Redemption! Sport? This can be addressed from the standpoint of Creation....but also by the Fall. Sickness and death? Genetic engineering? The Family? Art? Sex? The work ethic? Go on....*work it out*.

You will for ever be rounding off your settled view of our existence; you will never stop learning and improving. But from the earliest days, get these four planks in place – and amazingly you will already be knowing your way around. I have always felt this way about the Wimbledon tennis championships; I have been so often that it has become a part of me. When I was a student I even sold ice creams there one year. "You want the South-West entrance? Over there!....The Members' Enclosure? Fifty yards to the right!....The Wimbledon Museum? I'll take you!" I feel an ownership about the entire event. Paul the apostle writes in this style to new believers in Corinth – why, they even 'owned' the preachers who were helping them!

All things are yours, whether Paul or Apollos or Cephas or the world or life or death or the present or the future – all are yours; and you are Christ's; and Christ is God's (1 Corinthians 3:21-23).

The last phrase is vital. 'Christ' isn't yet one more of many leaders in our civilisation; he is part of the very Godhead. If you are 'Christ's', then in him you too have ownership in the universe of which he is centre. You can interpret life here. You know your way around. You do feel at home in this world – at last!

10

THE PATHWAY TO POWER

I was once invited to speak at the Christian Booksellers'
Convention in Blackpool. At its close the organisers very
kindly gave me rather a handsome pen with my name
inscribed on it. I took it home and then discovered that
I could not make it work. No ink flowed. I opened the
pen; there was no ink cartridge inside. Nor could I see any
cartridges inside the presentation box.

"They've given me this pen," I explained to a friend,
now in the publishing industry himself. "But it's got no
cartridges. It's a dud. Quite useless! All they've given me is
an inscribed metal tube!"

"Show me," said Rob Cook. He took the pen and
inspected it thoughtfully. "Now show me the box."

I rummaged in the wastebin and recovered the box.
Dutifully I handed it over. Rob opened it, and prised up a
little velvet cushion on which the pen had reposed.

"Voilà!" he exclaimed.

There underneath the cushion were six little shining ink
cartridges. They were only waiting to be used. The gift had
been good for use right from the start. I felt a little foolish.

When I think of the gift of Salvation, the reassurance
needs to be given swiftly; you can start to operate as an

effective Christian right away! For when God comes into our lives he does so comprehensively. We are not saved from the penalty of our sins, only to be told, "Ah, you haven't the complete equipment yet; that will have to come later."

"Cartridges to be acquired separately".... "Batteries not supplied" – this is not how the Christian life begins!

The power, the energy source for living a life that pleases God, is within us from the moment we receive the gift of forgiveness – *in the accompanying gift of the Holy Spirit*. Before his death, Jesus had told his disciples "I will not leave you as orphans; I will come to you" (John 14:18). He was referring to the day that would occur after his resurrection, only a few weeks later at the Jewish feast of Pentecost in Jerusalem. The Holy Spirit was to come in power upon the whole company of believers – Gentiles as well as Jews. Christ's words teach us that the coming of the Spirit would be equivalent to *his* coming into their lives. This wonderful event is recorded in Acts chapter 2. After the ascension of Jesus the disciples had been told to wait in Jerusalem until this promise was fulfilled.

By the time of Acts chapter 2, the waiting was over; it happened. It was dramatic; the sound of a rushing wind; the flames of fire above the heads of the disciples; the 'internationalising' of the church by the fact that on that miraculous inaugural day the onlookers were going to understand the preached words of the apostles, each in their own language! From that great landmark onwards, all believers in Christ everywhere would receive the promised Spirit, on their acceptance of the Gospel.

The thrilling news is not only that God, through the death and resurrection of Christ, will save us **from our**

past – but that, through the incoming worldwide tide of the Spirit of Pentecost, he has saved us **for the future**, for a life of service in this world. The tide has come in, on both Jewish and Gentile believers, from Pentecost onwards! We must understand that the apostolic preaching of the Gospel on that historic day in Jerusalem offered not one gift (the forgiveness of sins), but two! Here is Peter, preaching at Pentecost:

> *"Repent and be baptised, every one of you, in the name of Jesus Christ, for the **forgiveness** of your sins. And you will receive the **gift of the Holy Spirit**. The promise is for you and your children, and for all who are far off – for all whom the Lord our God will call." (Acts 2:38,39).*

It is fascinating to notice in the New Testament that, once we get past Pentecost, all the terms that describe what the Holy Spirit begins in the life of a Christian are spoken of as having already happened! Once we have put our trust in Christ and received forgiveness, we have been born again by the Spirit; we have *been anointed* by the Spirit; we *have been sealed* by the Spirit and *we have been baptised* in the Spirit.[1] Thus, none of these experiences are commanded upon us, once we have become disciples of Jesus – for these are all happenings connected with our initiation into Christ.

The only actual commands we are given about life in the Spirit relate to the *developing* of our Christian discipleship. "Don't quench the Spirit", we are told. "Walk

---

[1] For a full and wonderfully clear explanation on the Person and work of the Holy Spirit, see Billy Graham's book, *The Holy Spirit* (Word Books).

in the Spirit.... Pray in the Spirit.... Fight with spiritual weapons."

We are also commanded to be filled with the Holy Spirit (Ephesians 5:18). This could be translated, "Go on being filled with the Holy Spirit." It is to be a regular, indeed a daily occurrence. The full verse reads, "Do not get drunk on wine, which leads to debauchery. Instead, be filled with the Spirit." The apostle Paul is writing about two different kinds of control! *We are not to be controlled by alcohol; we are to be controlled by the Holy Spirit.*

How is it done? It is very simple. It involves no formula or technique. After all, we are speaking about a relationship with Jesus; what relationship ever needed a technique?

I remember, as a student, once attending a special missionary breakfast meeting. We were told that our visiting speaker had been instrumental, under God, at the very start of the mighty East African revival that has affected millions of people. The word went round that we were going to be hearing Dr Joe Church, 'a man filled with the Holy Ghost'. *Wow*! was the awed reaction.

But I had known 'Uncle' Joe from childhood, there in East Africa. A useful hockey player, he had been at college with my Dad. His part in the revival was perfectly true, but it was difficult to reconcile the public descriptions of the 'Holy Ghost' visionary with the family friend we had grown up with.

So when Joe Church turned up he seemed, with his toothbrush moustache, just the same approachable person I had always known. Sure, he was fine in every way! But by his appearance he could have been a bank clerk. And his speaking? It was, well....*okay*. But there were no gimlet eyes boring into us. No fireworks. It was remarkably 'natural'. He spoke hardly at all about the Holy Spirit; it was all about Jesus.

A Christian controlled by the Holy Spirit is essentially Christ-centred and Christ-aware. You don't have to go to a special meeting in order to be filled with the Holy Spirit. Your face doesn't have to glow; you aren't required to speak in a special tone of voice!

If there is no 'technique' required for the Spirit of Christ to fill his followers, are there at least some helpful guidelines? We can be sure there are.

Remove the blockages

In our relationship with the Lord, day by day we can come to him and ask him to remove from our lives those things that would otherwise block his fullness in us. By daily repentance we are to see to it that the sins we are aware of are dealt with at the Cross. Of course we know that we were justified and forgiven *for ever* when we first trusted Christ. We were then adopted into the family of God as sons and daughters. Nothing can change that; it is permanent. If a little boy throws a ball through the front window of his parents' home, relations will be strained for a while! But they are not *ended*; he is still the child of his parents. So it is in our walk with God. What we are looking for is an undisturbed relationship with the indwelling Lord of our lives.

This matches with an earlier observation that the Cross is our way of life. The death and resurrection of Jesus are never far away from the Christian. In our continuing gratitude for all that happened at the Cross of Calvary, we shall frequently be aware of our sins that put Christ there, and we shall want to have them out of our lifestyle. As we do this on a daily basis, so the blockages to his infilling are removed, and the pathway to power is cleared.

Obey the Lord

It is an obvious point to observe. Amazingly, Christ desires to make his home in the life of a Christian. It all began that day when his voice was heard, and the door was opened to the indwelling Spirit. On top of this, he wishes to fill and fulfil every part of the residence that is my life. It is, then, as I continue to surrender to him in obedience – as Lord of my life every day – that I can expect him to fill my whole being with his presence and power.

This means taking his words and his commands seriously. Jesus emphasised the desirability of a clean home in our lives!

> *If anyone loves me, he will obey my teaching. My Father will love him, and we will come to him and make our home with him (John 14:23).*

The closeness of both Father and Son is brought home to the heart of an obedient believer through the work of the infilling Spirit. It is interesting to notice that in Paul's letter to the Colossians – so much a 'parallel' to the similar letter to the Ephesians – we are urged not so much to let the Spirit fill us, as to 'Let the word of Christ dwell in you richly' (Colossians 3:16). *It amounts to the same thing.* To be taking in and obeying Christ's word 'richly' means that we are going to be filled with his Spirit! Obey his word. Make him Lord. And he will fill you! But here is a third guideline:

Share your blessings

It sounds contradictory – and indeed it is a surprise for us to learn this truth – *the way to be filled is to be emptied.* The reason is that the filling of the Holy Spirit was never given simply to make us feel good; he fills us so that in lifestyle, by character (the 'fruit' of the Spirit – Galatians 5:22), and through downright energetic service we can be powerful witnesses to the ends of the earth. Pentecost had yet to take place when Jesus explained to his disciples the source of power that would energise his world mission:

> *But you will receive power when the Holy Spirit comes on you; and you will be my witnesses in Jerusalem, and in all Judea and Samaria, and to the ends of the earth (Acts 1:8).*

Try it out! It is as we launch out in Christian service that we can believe the necessary power will be given. The principle seems to be twofold:

> *Obeying, not waiting*
> *Sharing, not hoarding*

You can prove this yourself. You will take on some demanding piece of service for the Lord, and you will make the discovery that *in the doing of it* you are being filled and assisted. Afterwards someone will say, "You must be feeling very tired, very drained." The contrary is more likely to be true. You will find to your amazement that you feel better, more refreshed, fulfilled and invigorated at the end of the assignment than you did at the beginning. We can relate this to the filling of the Holy Spirit. As we share our blessings, God himself moves in and fills us.

Remove the blockages....Obey the Lord....Share your blessings. Here is the pathway to power. It's exciting and practical; yet a further question that many believers will ask is "**How can I KNOW that I am filled with the Spirit?**" We can close off this chapter with three simple, yet life-changing observations that tie in with what we have already learnt.

The Spirit-filled Christian is more aware of Christ than of the Holy Spirit. There is this strange anonymity about the Spirit of God. He is not given to us, in order to draw attention to himself, but to Christ. Jesus said, about the Holy Spirit,

> *"He will bring glory to me, by taking from what is mine, and making it known to you" (John 16:14).*

I have sometimes been asked, "Is yours a Holy Spirit church?" You can only answer that question by asking another question, *What place does CHRIST have in our church*? It is the work of the Spirit to throw floods of light on Jesus!

How then can we know that we are filled with the Spirit? Ask another question! How central is Jesus Christ to your life? The answer lies there.

The Spirit-filled Christian is more concerned with emptying than with filling. We can sometimes delude ourselves into thinking that the experience of being filled with the Holy Spirit is an added-value 'extra' to Christian living, involving sensational preachers, thrilling books and tapes, special conferences and dramatic late-night meetings!

Naturally, conferences, books and videos all have their use.[2] But we are not required to find God and his blessings through fantastic experiences, or by travelling to some kind of Christian equivalent to Mecca – so central to Muslims. The whole point of the Bible's message is the wonderful disclosure that *he* comes to *us*, there in the hospital, in the refugee camp, in prison, right at the bedside as we wake up to a new day. *Being filled with the Spirit involves us in using the gifts God has given us, in obedient out-going service*, in the confident belief that as we empty ourselves, the Spirit will equip and empower us. Indeed Spirit-filled servants of the Lord are not really thinking about themselves at all – owing to their desire to be of help to others.

So the filling of the Holy Spirit is not to be hugged to ourselves; nor – interestingly – even to be testified about publicly. Nowhere in the New Testament do we read of individuals declaring "I am filled with the Holy Spirit." It was always left to *others* to make the observation as to whether a particular individual was filled with the Spirit. *Lesson*: If you are ever asked, "Have you been filled with the Spirit?" the appropriate answer is, "Ask my family – they'll tell you!" "Better ask my boss!"

The Spirit-filled Christian is more concerned with the moral than the sensational. We have an illustration from the Corinthian church of Paul's time. They were fascinated by the whole realm of the supernatural and the miraculous; yet Paul had to describe them as 'worldly', as mere 'infants', because of the sexual immorality found within their membership. Where was the Christlikeness

---

[2] For a helpful video/dvd study for housegroups and seminars, see No 4, 'The Holy Spirit', from the *Open Home, Open Bible* programme: (Ref. ZX324). Enquiries: www.allsouls.org (Tel. 020 7612 9773); For USA: www.visionvideo.com

of character? The entire Christian witness is a sham if that is missing.

How can I know that I am filled with the Spirit? If, in fact, we are genuinely caught up in the life of the Holy Spirit, we shall be so occupied with the interests of God's kingdom and with the needs of others that we will forget we ever asked the question.

But ask to be filled, every day! And believe, as you roll out of bed, that everything you do in the day ahead is going to be touched with the indwelling power of God himself.

11

APPROVED BY GOD

As a student, I remember once being coached at tennis by none other than the famous Dan Maskell. It was rather an honour to have our top British coach come to our university courts – and then for as limited a player as I knew myself to be to have my own session with him for forty minutes. How much I wanted to please him! To show off my best shots – keen, as a young tennis hopeful, to gain his endorsement! In fact he bequeathed to me a new service action, which I was to use ever afterwards. I've always been grateful for my 'Dan Maskell serve'. I hope I'm a credit to his memory. When you are with such a coach you covet their approval.

Back in AD 67 the apostle Paul was writing like an older 'coach' to his younger protégé Timothy. Yet if Paul was the coach, it's evident from this second of two letters, that Timothy was being urged to gain the approval not simply of the coach, but of the one who had first picked up Paul, those many years ago on the Damascus Road – the Lord himself:

> *Do your best to present yourself to God as one approved (2 Timothy 2:15).*

The second letter to Timothy, written from prison, features a galaxy of names. They were of people noted, either for being useful to God, or deserving of the ash heap. There were Timothy's grandmother Lois and his mother Eunice – names honoured along with such as Onesiphorus and Titus, Luke and Tychicus. In contrast we read of Phygellus and Hermogenes, or Hymenaeus and Philetus – individuals who got themselves into the Bible for their uselessness in the cause of the Gospel. It can be said that there are two kinds of people in the world; those who are consumers only – out to grab anything and everything for themselves – and those who are contributors.

As one approved.... It becomes pointed and very personal for Timothy. It is possible that he had been won to faith in Christ during a mission led by Paul in Lystra around the year AD 47 (Acts 14:8-20). Certainly by the time of Paul's next visit to the city Timothy is a disciple (Acts 16:1,2). Now he is a church leader and a worker. [1]

Could that describe you....or is it going to be you? It need not take long for this very thing to happen! Much depends on how hungry an individual is for the things of God and his service. Several descriptions of the effective Christian emerge from this glowing letter of Paul's – and they still inspire us today.

The approved worker – getting the word right

Read it in full: *Do your best to present yourself to God as one approved, a workman who does not need to be ashamed,*

[1] For useful further study, see *2 Timothy* in the 'Book by Book' video/dvd series, featuring Bible teacher Vaughan Roberts with Paul Blackham and Richard Bewes. Enquiries: www.allsouls.org (Tel: 020 7612 9773). USA: www.visionvideo.com

and who correctly handles the word of truth. These letters of 1 and 2 Timothy, together with the letter to Titus, are called *The Pastoral Letters*, because they deal – for the most part – with the requirements to be found in the Christian minister or worker. May these centuries-old words of Paul inspire us to become established workers for the kingdom of Jesus Christ! Give it three…. five years – and it could well be that you won't recognise yourself in the things that you have been able to take on, in the life of the church.

The foundational equipment relates to the Scriptures and our attitude to them. "*Cutting straight* the word of truth" is the literal translation from the Greek of 2 Timothy 2:15. *Implication*: we are not to twist God's word and so bring 'ruin' (the Greek word is *katastrophe* – verse 14) to the listeners, nor are we to blunt its cutting edge with pointless arguments about divisive issues, or what verse 16 calls 'godless chatter'.

All down Christian history we have known of such things taking place. Trivial deviations and the latest fads have taken their toll within widespread areas of church life. The pattern of false teaching is predictable; first it *dazzles*, then it *distorts*, next it *diverts* and finally it *destroys*.

"Have you heard of the amazing new thing that's happening over in Ephesus? These new preachers, Hymenaeus and Philetus – they're awesome; they're better than Paul; in fact they've gone beyond him!"

"I don't know why you keep on sticking with that old church where you first began. Come over to *us* – you've never heard anyone like Phygelus and Hermogenes!"

The apostle Paul is very firm about any movement that fails to cut the word of God straight. Their teaching spreads "like gangrene" (v.17). These are workers "who have wandered away from the truth" (v.16). Result, *catastrophe*. It's the old principle of the angle. Get your understanding of God's word half a degree away from true – and at first there may seem to be no appreciable difference in your belief. However, you have only to travel ten years down the track, uncorrected – and you will be a chasm away from the given truth of Christ and his apostles – and never even realise it.

It is for this reason that any training undertaken in Christian service needs a firm underlay of Bible understanding from the start. A student group, a church seminar, a correspondence course or video/dvd programme – over the years I have observed that the workers for God who take advantage of such study become equipped, with amazing and rapid results. They leave the rest far behind.

The apostle gives to his trainee Timothy another portrait of the effective Christian servant:

The clean utensil – getting the character right

Paul visualises the church of God as a large household that needs to be run properly. Within it are many articles; vessels and cups, pieces of crockery, chairs and ornaments. It is a vivid piece of imagery. Where do you fit into this picture?

> *In a large house there are articles not only of gold and silver, but also of wood and clay; some are for noble purposes and some for ignoble. If a man cleanses himself from the latter, he will be an instrument for noble purposes, made holy, useful to the Master and prepared to do any good work (2 Timothy 2:20,21).*

This stately mansion contains objects both ornate and simple. Look at that beautiful silver salver…. and the gold clock that chimes so prettily! But I can see a wooden kitchen table, around which a family will sit. There is also an earthenware crock that keeps the bread fresh. Utensils, vessels and 'instruments' as Paul calls them – they all have a use.

At the Church of All Souls, Langham Place, a gift was once made publicly to visiting preacher Billy Graham. It was a piece of Wedgwood fine art – a blue porcelain mug with the Church of All Souls embossed on one side. *But did it have any use?* It was later, on a visit to the USA, that I happened to see the mug. It had been placed on a desk. It was crammed with ballpoints, crayons and rubber bands. I said nothing, but I thought, *He's found a use for it.*

Many of the 'articles' – or people – that are found within God's household fulfil a noble purpose, explains Paul. But some of them are 'ignoble'. By this, the apostle is not referring to 'humble' or 'menial' purposes, as might be attributed to the worthy wooden spoon. *Ignoble*, in the original Greek, comes from the same root word used in Romans 1:26, for '*shameful* lusts'.

We must apply this to the household of God's church. Some of its human instruments or vessels might be given a prominent 'on show' role. Others might serve a less visible yet essential purpose. What gives the utensil its 'nobility' is neither glamour nor size, but its *cleanliness*. 'If a man cleanses himself' (v.21) – that is the determining factor! *Are we clean?* At the very least, are we intending to be clean? If we are, then we are called 'holy, useful to the Master and prepared to do any good work'.

Cleanliness of character is fairly easy to fake, yet

we cannot fool God. He knows exactly what a man or woman is really like. But he also knows whether we are at least engaged in *battle*, for holiness of living. This being so, he can incorporate into his service every one of us who persist in the struggle. What matters most is where the heart is focused.

Alf Stanway, a robust Anglican bishop from Melbourne, spent much of his Christian ministry in dusty Tanzania. Later he became the first Principal of the Trinity Episcopal School of Ministry in Pittsburgh. At his inaugural speech he encouraged his younger colleagues:

> *If other people knew you, like God knows you; all your faults and all your thoughts, all your sins, all the things in your heart that have been in there; all the wrong thoughts that you've ever had – would they trust you with the kind of work that God trusts you with? Here is the supreme confidence that God has in his own grace. He'll take the likes of you and me, and give you the privilege of being his servants. He's got to take people like you and me. He has no others.*

If it is a clean heart and character that we are pursuing, God will use us!

Here now is Paul's third portrait of the effective Christian worker:

The fruitful servant – getting others right

Bringing others into the family of believers is not a highly skilled exercise. It is, rather, a way of life for anyone who has been captivated by the love of God in Jesus Christ. I got to know a London businessman called Vijay Menon many years ago. Converted to Christ, during a lunchtime service at St Helen's Church in Bishopsgate, he never looked back. He stayed in his company as a layman, he was never on the paid staff of any church – but the joy of knowing that his sins were forgiven prompted him to want to win others, just as he had been won.

It began with one other person. Then another. Then his wife. After a while Vijay was able to stand up in public and tell his story of coming to know Christ. He developed the habit of getting alongside his friends, yes, and strangers too. People warmed to his infectious enthusiasm and to his lively Bible talks. He began to be in demand. It began to be asked, "How many people has Vijay won to faith?" We lost count when it was running into hundreds.... then thousands!

The immediate reaction is, "I could never do that." Yet the target is not thousands. The target is one. Remember Augustine? "One loving spirit sets another on fire." Paul's word-picture of the fruitful servant of Christ is an attractive one:

> *And the Lord's servant must not quarrel; instead he must be kind to everyone, able to teach, not resentful. Those who oppose him he must gently instruct, in the hope that God will grant them repentance leading them to a knowledge of the truth, and that they will come to their senses and escape from the trap of the devil, who has taken them captive to do his will (2 Timothy 2:24-26).*

At times God's people must indeed engage in controversy, but essentially we were not called to 'quarrel', but to be productive; not to be disputers but messengers! This can happen on the level of the student campus, the family, work colleagues, or neighbours and friends.

On a trip to one of our English cities I met an ex-con man. He had swindled many companies out of thousands of pounds. In his flat, however, he became aware of the consistent lifestyle of two neighbours, both young men, who attended church every Sunday evening. One day he spoke to them:

"That place you go to on Sunday evenings…. Could you ever get me a ticket?"

The two young men played it cool. They held back from telling Fred that church was free.

"Leave it to us, Fred. We'll see what we can do."

Sunday arrived.

"It's all fixed, Fred. We're going tonight. Come along!"

There, in Anglican evening service, sat the con man between his two neighbours. My brother-in-law, Gordon Bridger, was the preacher. Fred became a follower of Christ that very night. Then he had to go to the police and straighten out his life. But that is another story.

What had the two young men done to get another person right? *Nothing*. They had simply been there as humble, consistent servants of Christ. But in doing so they had pulled a man out of a life of crime and into the eternal kingdom of God. That is fruitfulness!

Anything you want me to do for you today, Lord? Well, I'm here at your service. Just for you.

To be on hand for Him – as the approved worker, as the clean utensil, as the fruitful servant – any and every day can begin in this way, with one aim; *to please*, to be approved by God.

12

EATING – AND REMEMBERING

If you were to take some visitors from outer space and confront them with the great pyramids of Egypt, they could hardly fail to exclaim, "What are they? What are they *for*?" Their towering structures dominate all else. The same is true of Nelson's Column, the George Washington Monument or the Eiffel Tower.

Some of these great monuments are tombs, commemorating the mighty leaders of history. But for Jesus there is no tomb. The man who towers over all others, who divides civilisation into BC and AD, left no memorial. He never even wrote a book. All he did – by which he could be remembered – was to take bread and wine on the eve of his death and distribute it among his few friends. "Eat this…. drink this…. in remembrance of me," he directed them.

Since then, for centuries, wherever Jesus' followers are found, we have been following these commands. "But why?" a stranger might ask. "What does it mean?"

Centuries before Jesus was born, the same question was being asked about the Israelite feast of the Passover. In the words of Moses:

And when your children ask you, 'What does this ceremony mean to you?' then tell them, 'It is the Passover sacrifice to the LORD, who passed over the houses of the Israelites in Egypt and spared our homes when he struck down the Egyptians' (Exodus 12:26,27).

Give yourself a few minutes to think about the bread and the cup of the Jesus 'meal', and its remarkable link with the ancient feast of the Jewish Passover. For you and I – if we know Jesus at all – will be sharing in this service of remembrance not once nor twice, but on scores, even hundreds of occasions. First of all, when was it instituted?

This is significant. The New Testament record informs us:

'Then came the day of Unleavened Bread on which the Passover lamb had to be sacrificed. Jesus sent Peter and John, saying, "Go and make preparations for us to eat the Passover" (Luke 22:7,8).

Ever since the people of Israel had been delivered out of Egypt under the leadership of Moses, the Passover had been held to commemorate this great act of deliverance. On that dramatic evening, the enslaved Israelites prepared to leave the land of their oppression, with a special sacrificial offering of a lamb. This was to be eaten with bitter herbs – a reminder of the bitterness of their past oppression. The blood from the sacrifice was to be applied to the sides and tops of their doorposts.

It was a night of divine judgement on the houses of the Egyptians, as death struck at every household. But the Israelite households were to be spared. The warning to them was stark:

*"The blood will be a sign for you on the houses where you
are; and when I see the blood, I will pass over you. No
destructive plague will touch you when I strike Egypt"
(Exodus 12:13).*

It was the beginning of freedom from tyranny for
God's people.

Here was a landmark event in the renewing of what
was called the 'Covenant', a pledged relationship between
God and Israel – and God's people would forever be
reminded of it in future Passover celebrations.

Now, centuries later, Christ's disciples found themselves
on the threshold of a greater and universal act of deliverance
– the saving death of Jesus – *and it was Passover time*. This
was no coincidence; Jesus had clearly planned to institute
his Supper as a new form of Passover. That Thursday
evening was a *transition* night between the old and the
new order. It is a pity that many church members take
part in the Holy Communion without ever having been
informed about its background of the Passover.

The Passover proceedings were as follows. After prayer,
the head of the house passed round a cup of wine with
the words, *Blessed be thou, O Lord our God, King of the
world, who hast created the fruit of the Vine*. Next, there
passed from one to the other a kind of salad of bitter
herbs – the age-old reminder of the oppression in the
book of Exodus. The herbs were eaten after being dipped
in a sauce made up of almonds, nuts, figs and other fruits
– the sauce itself being red in colour, as a reminder of
the hard labour of brick-making imposed by the former
Egyptian taskmasters.

Then a second cup was passed round, and the meaning

of the Passover was explained by the household leader. Two unleavened loaves or cakes were then taken; one of them was broken, and the pieces placed above each other. With a prayer of thanks, one of the pieces would then be dipped in the sauce and eaten, along with part of the sacrificial lamb and the herbs. Everyone would follow suit.

A third cup followed – 'the cup of blessing', as it was called – and this was accompanied by a prayer of thanks from the leader. Then a fourth cup was distributed. Following that, a hymn would be sung (see Psalms 113–118). Sometimes even a fifth cup would be added, together with further singing from Psalms 120–127.

Have you followed, up to now? On that solemn night in an upper room, Jesus was *transforming* the Passover as he went along, and so instituting between God and his people a 'covenant' that was new – yet linked to the old.

> *And he took bread, gave thanks and broke it, and gave it to them, saying, "This is my body given for you; do this in remembrance of me." In the same way, after the supper, he took the cup, saying, "This cup is the new covenant in my blood, which is poured out for you" (Luke 22:19,20).*

Here now was a different service, built on the old, but with a new idea at its heart – the sacrificial death of a lamb who was none other than 'The Lamb of God' the person of Jesus himself. It commemorated a new deliverance, a 'new covenant', a new order altogether – and the apostle Paul was aware of this in a phrase written to his Christian friends,

"For Christ, our Passover lamb, has been sacrificed. Therefore let us keep the Festival…." (1 Corinthians 5:7).

The Holy Communion takes different forms, according to culture and tradition – but basically what we do in this service goes right back to that upper-room Supper. Where is the emphasis to be placed? What are we supposed to be thinking? We can look at it in five different ways.

The backward look – we commemorate

"Do this in remembrance of me." But why? The reason is plain – we forget too easily. Supposing that there was no observance of the Lord's Supper? Over the years we might well feel inclined to merge the death of Jesus with all the other great New Testament events; to say, in effect, "Of course the cross was important, but so were Christ's baptism, the healings and teaching, and the great example of his life."

We could go further, and recognise that some of us recoil from the concept of *blood*; we shrink from focusing on something so 'primitive' in our sophisticated era. But the Lord's Supper leads us inescapably to the importance of the cross as absolutely central in the life of a believer. We are to eat, drink – *and remember what it cost for us to be forgiven.*

We look *back* to that one great sacrifice for sin. It can never be repeated. Although, in the Holy Communion, we are dramatising what Christ has done for us, in no sense can Christ ever be offered again for our sins. For it is a *table* that we now come before, at the Communion – not an altar! An altar is for sacrifices, but the unique sacrifice for sins has already been made, once for all

– never to be repeated in any way (Hebrews 9:25-28). We are wise, then, to follow the example of the Anglican Book of Common Prayer. In it – and in its revisions – no mention is made of an 'altar' – despite much careless use of such a phrase in some circles. The Lord's Supper helps us to look back to what Christ has done, *once*…. and we remember this with our heartfelt thanks.

The upward look – we communicate

However, it is not a dead Saviour that we worship and commune with, when we meet in this way. Our Master is alive – and as we read the Scriptures and hear them explained; as we sing and pray, and then receive the symbols of bread and wine, we are irresistibly reminded of his love and of his risen presence among us, and we are drawn closer to him.

It is not that there is intrinsic power in the bread and cup, as such. The Communion is one of two 'Sacraments of the Gospel' (the other being Baptism).[1] Here is a Gospel 'visual aid', dramatizing the historical fact of the body and blood of Jesus given for us in a violent death. The bread and wine are the outward symbols of an inward and spiritual reality – namely, feeding upon the Lord by faith in our hearts. No superstition should be attached to these visible symbols. They remain simply bread and wine; they are not to be the objects of people's adoration, as sometimes occurs.

And yet they are powerful symbols! Just as a photograph

---

[1] See programme 6 in the *Open Home, Open Bible* video/dvd series on 'The Church' (ZX 330). www.allsouls.org (Tel 020 7612 9773). USA – www.visionvideo.com

will provide a reminder of a loved one – and even seem to bring them a little closer – so it is with the symbolism of the Lord's Supper. The theologians call this *dynamic symbolism*. We are communicating with the risen Lord – and he with us – at the Lord's Table. Result – we fall in love with him again, we are reassured of his pledged presence with us, and so are revitalized. It is a *Communion* with him.

The inward look – we appropriate

The body of Christ…. The blood of Christ…. Eat this…. drink this. We can understand that these are figurative terms. The bread *represents* Christ's body to us. That is the whole point of a sacrament. It is the outward and visible symbol (the bread and wine) of an inward and spiritual reality (being forgiven and purified at the Cross).

But for some there is a problem. "It sounds too horrible," they say. "It sounds primitive and so strange to modern ears. *Eating Christ's flesh, drinking his blood*. What am I supposed to be thinking when I use such terms?"

The Bible's own use of imagery helps us at this point. In traditional Jewish thinking, to 'eat the flesh' or 'drink the blood' of someone meant to take advantage of their death or their downfall. The psalmist of old spoke of his enemies who 'came upon me to eat up my flesh' (Psalm 27:2 rsv). What did he mean? He meant that evildoers intended to take advantage of him! A similar phrase occurs in the account of three brave soldiers who risked their lives to obtain water from the well of Bethlehem for King David. Overwhelmed at their exploits through enemy-held territory, David poured out the cup of precious water on the ground as a thank-offering to the Lord, and refused to drink.

> *Far be it from me, O LORD, that I should do this. Shall I*
> *drink the blood of the men who went at the risk of their*
> *lives? (2 Samuel 23:17 RSV).*

Such a phrase could only mean one thing. David felt unable to take advantage of the possible death of the three heroes.

We can now more easily apply the term to ourselves. *The day we accepted Christ into our lives we were, by faith, taking advantage of his death for us.* Jesus used these very terms, to describe the believer's trust in himself.

> *"I tell you the truth, unless you eat the flesh of the Son of*
> *Man and drink his blood, you have no life in you. Whoever*
> *eats my flesh and drinks my blood has eternal life, and I*
> *will raise him up at the last day" (John 6:53,54).*

To 'eat' and 'drink', then, is to take advantage of Christ's death for your sins and to believe in him.

We are symbolising this in the Lord's Supper, as we partake of the bread and drink from the cup. In doing so we are reminding ourselves once more of the death at Calvary and of our participation in it. These visible emblems help us to take it in again; of what it means to be justified, forgiven, liberated and accepted into the family of God. *Does he love me? Did he really save me?* The bread and the cup tell me, 'He does! He did!' In that moment of intimacy with the Lord, we are appropriating afresh the blessings he has won for us by his sacrifice. We are taking advantage of his death – and Calvary seems to be very close.

For new believers this is very powerful. Naturally, some

training in understanding is right and helpful before regular participation is expected at Communion. In Anglican or Episcopal churches it is common to provide classes to prepare younger members – or new converts to Christ – for *confirmation* as full 'communicant' members of the fellowship. Every church will have its own procedures for training in membership.

Yet there is nothing that should prevent the newest member of the saved community from taking part in the Lord's Supper, if we are true to the Gospel. I have known some to take part even before they were baptised. It is only a concern for some rounded Bible understanding and for an ordered church life that prompts us – as a norm – to regularise our patterns of membership.

The outward look – we participate

"Take this," said Jesus, "and divide it among yourselves" (Luke 22:17 RSV).

From the start we can recognise that the Lord's Supper was not a private and individualistic affair; it was a family gathering, a sharing. The apostle Paul called it a 'participation' in the body and blood of Christ (1 Corinthians 10:16,17). He reminded his readers that, just as the many pieces of broken bread all came from the one loaf, so we all, though many people, are one body in Christ. We belong to each other.

Grudges, then, are not to be harboured among Christians who share in this family occasion. We are wise to examine ourselves before taking part. *Am I in love and harmony with my fellow-believers? Is there something that needs to be put right between myself and another, before sharing with my friends from the same loaf?*

It is not that we come to the Lord's table as squeaky-clean paragons of virtue! Unworthy sinners we will always know ourselves to be – and it is this very knowledge that brings us together in renewed repentance, yet in grateful trust. Stockbrokers and factory-hands, teenagers and senior citizens, senators, janitors and computer analysts; all these categories fade to nothing – at the foot of the cross!

The forward look – we anticipate

The Lord's Supper has a time limit fixed upon it. We shall not be holding these services after Christ returns! For then our communion with him will be direct, face to face. In the meantime his presence and his love are mediated to us in a number of ways, and what better way than through the simple remembrance meal that he commanded us to observe? But not for ever:

> *For whenever you eat this bread and drink this cup, you proclaim the Lord's death until he comes (1 Corinthians 11:26).*

One day… he'll be back. In a strange way the Supper which seems, on first evidence, to be pointing backwards is also a signpost to the future, to Christ's glorious return; to what the book of Revelation calls 'the marriage supper of the Lamb'.

Value the Holy Communion then. It is not necessarily the most *frequently* held main service in the life of a church, for it is essentially intended for the family of believers – and the healthy church is the one which, in its regular services, is also vigorous in Bible teaching and evangelism, reaching out to an untaught society. But the Lord's Supper will always be loved by Gospel people.

Indeed, at times of spiritual awakening, the services of Holy Communion have been known to overspill out of the church, and under the trees, so great has been the press of eager participants. When the Wesley brothers and George Whitefield were preaching two hundred and fifty years ago, they would sometimes hold a service of Communion out in the open fields. In a crowd of twenty or thirty thousand, perhaps only the first three thousand or so would get to participate in the bread and the cup. But did that matter? All knew that they had been present for a never-to-be-forgotten occasion!

Whether it is in church, in a great cathedral or in a simple dwelling within the cattle economy of a developing nation, people who love Christ feel their hearts tugged in a special way as they obey the summons of two thousand years ago, 'Do this, in remembrance of me.'

13

THE WINNING SIDE

"I'm terribly sorry, Lord, but I'm going to have a double whisky."

Frank was the chief executive of the company that bore his name, for he had been its creator; his product was in every supermarket. But he was an alcoholic. Weeks earlier he had been born again as a new Christian, during a mission in Greater London. Now the struggle was on to break with his drink habit.

"There's nothing I can do about it," Frank prayed, as he walked the street. "I feel bad about it, Lord, but I simply have to have a double whisky."

He reached the pub and went in. The barman greeted him:

"What will it be then?"

"At that point," related Frank later, "I heard myself say, 'I'd like a glass of lemonade, please!'"

No, it wasn't a cure. Plenty of further battles would lie ahead. But it was a reassuring moment of grace in the Christian life of a new believer.

This is the point of it all. The possibility of winning is scarcely in our mindset when first stepping out in discipleship. We had come to take sinful habits and attitudes for granted. We were one-dimensional people, geared to this life alone; trapped by materialism, living for ourselves. Indeed we were so helpless that we had no idea of our predicament.

Then one day the picture changed. The Liberator came! He sliced through those bonds that held us captive, and threw them into the fireplace. He scooped up the heavy weights of guilt that had anchored us to the floor, and tossed them out of the window. He picked up a heavy iron poker lying in the corner, and said, "See that intruder at the door? That's your opponent the devil. I want you to take this, and go and deal with him."

We hesitate

"Great Liberator, can't you go? You're so much stronger!"

"No," comes the reply. "I dealt with him a long time ago, on a hilltop; he knows he's beaten. Now it's your turn. *Go in and win.*"

An amazing thing happens as we take up our weapons. We discover that when we resist wrongdoing and evil – as we deliberately choose Christ and his standards – the opposition gives way. We obey the advice of James 4:7, to resist the devil, and discover to our astonishment that he 'flees' from us, and that we are able 'to beat down Satan under our feet'!

But who is Satan? He is evidently part of the created angelic order. The angels were not created as evil beings, for everything in God's creation was good. But there is enough in the Bible to indicate that part of the angelic world, headed by Satan, chose to rebel against the divine authority, and so fell (2 Peter 2:1; Jude 6). Humanity – as headed by its representatives, Adam and Eve – colluded in the rebellion, and in this way evil entered into the world. Augustine of old explained it thus:

> *The evil angels, though created good, became evil by their voluntary defection from the good, so that the cause of evil is not the good but defection from the good.*[1]

The kingdom of evil, then, is headed by Satan, a powerful being indeed – but not on a level with God. The Bible never teaches what is called Dualism; God and the devil are not co-equal or co-existent. Satan is not divine, he has no independent existence, he is not all-knowing and he has a limited existence. It was at the cross that the satanic 'powers and authorities' lost their essential hold (Colossians 2:15), so guaranteeing the devil's final destruction. We may wonder why the devil's very presence is not eliminated already….until we remember that, when he is destroyed, his whole kingdom goes with him – and that could include a great many people that can yet be 'snatched' from his power (Jude 23). It is owing to the patience of the Lord – who wants everybody to come to repentance – that the end has not yet come (2 Peter 3:9).

What we see in the power of evil today, then, are not the pulsating vibrations of a kingdom in ascendancy, but the thrashing death-throes of a kingdom in desperation! I once saw a barracuda fish that had just been caught off the East African coast. With its snapping jaws, you could lose a finger if you got too close! So with the devil and all his works. He is doomed to destruction, but keep your distance while his end approaches!

---

[1] *The City of God*, Book 12.

Through a spell-binding array of stratagems and deceptions, the power of evil is exerted on every continent. We must not be surprised if, in making friends with Christ, we discover that we have also made a great enemy.

> *Be self-controlled and alert. Your enemy the devil prowls around like a roaring lion looking for someone to devour. Resist him, standing firm in the faith, because you know that your brothers throughout the world are undergoing the same kind of sufferings (1 Peter 5:8).*

Open the New Testament where you will; the same wonderful theme is woven into it. Christ is the great winner, while death, darkness and evil must retreat as the great losers. As we identify with our Lord and choose his side, so his victory – won at the cross – becomes our victory.

"Now that you've changed sides," I once said to a new Christian, "you're like the newly naturalised Frenchman who was asked how he felt on becoming English. 'Ah, *mon ami*,' he replied, 'that is simple. Waterloo used to be a great defeat. Now it has become a victory!'"

But let us be practical. *What do you **do** when you are tempted?* Those old habits and outlooks, that explosive temper; swearing and scandalmongering, the gossip and the lying; the cutting of corners, the relentless pressure on sexual standards, the vanities, excesses and ingrained self-promotion? We must remember the statement of James 1:13, that God is not the author of temptation. If he permits us to be tempted, it is so that we will gain in spiritual strength by resisting – as well as by learning from our mistakes. Temptation in itself is not sin, for Jesus himself was tempted.

Sometimes we can almost unconsciously engage in a little 'double-think' when we fall to temptation, convincing ourselves that 'the devil was too strong for me'. But his power against the believer is limited to temptation alone. We cannot be coerced into sinning. Further, we need to be reminded that there are three pressures – not simply one – exerted against us. They are *the world and the flesh* as well as the devil. 'The world' is the entire body of outlook that limits life to what can be seen, possessed and indulged in. 'The flesh' is that part of me which is governed by my inner, selfish appetites and desires.

Beware, then, of the extremist line of teaching that lumps the three categories – the world, the flesh and the devil – into a single camp, that of the devil alone! Then the untaught, in particular, can fall prey to the suggestion that their sinful habits are due to an evil spirit that must be thrown out of them by specialist 'deliverance' counselling. This can result in terrible confusion. Certainly we ministers from time to time will be required to counsel individuals with an occult history, but that is very different from the plain fact that, when we fall to temptation, it is because – in submitting to the desires of 'the flesh' – *we chose to sin!*

Further, it is no use our complaining that we were not given 'power' to resist – for we had all the power of the indwelling Spirit available.

It is not that at certain points we *cannot* win; it is that all too often we do not *want* to win; we find it personally too inconvenient to say No. The issue is almost entirely one of **motivation**.

*What do you **do** when you are tempted?* was our earlier question. This is a question that affects the plumber and the politician, the scientist and the student. It raises issues that must be addressed and worked on, in boardroom and bedroom alike. We can share the secrets of Christian victory with some simple maxims:

Stay in the fight

Some of us don't even fight, when it comes to resisting the downward pull of unbelieving society. Having caved in we then stay on the ground, dismally signalling for the ambulance to arrive! Failure seems built into our thinking: *Am I alone in my struggles? Have all these awesomely successful Christians left me at the starting gate? What a useless person I am! Who can get me out of this rut?*

But we can take comfort from the words of the apostle Paul – writing as an advanced believer:

> *What a wretched man I am! Who will rescue me from this body of death? (Romans 7:24).*

If Paul himself felt the tension of engaging in the battle for purity of life, it should come as no great surprise that others will feel the same. True, it is a fight; we were promised nothing less when we started out on the Christian road. What makes the experience liveable is, firstly, that *Christianity is true*, and secondly, that *we are in a state of friendship with God, forever*. Besides these things, nothing else matters; the fight, the inconvenience, the setbacks, even! In Christ we are accepted, exactly as we are, failure rate and all. It is this knowledge that motivates us to please him – and stay in the fight.

There will be occasions when, for the hundredth time, we fail – and then seem to hear that insidious whisper.

'Call yourself a Christian? You're a fine one to ask for forgiveness – you said that only yesterday….*and* the day before!' It is a common New Testament experience for the disciples of Christ to discover within them ever further levels of sin, the more they progress.

When our family lived in the South East of London, we teenagers were promised sixpence for every bucketful of pebbles that we were able to remove from our garden. The payments had to cease when a neighbour kindly informed Dad that our home was situated right above the Blackheath pebble bed, one hundred feet thick!

How many sins are there to be excavated from our fallen human nature? They will go on coming to light until we die! Thus the Gospel's working in our lives is not one of the total *eradication* of our sinfulness this side of the grave. It is rather one of *counteraction*. The challenge of Christian living is that we are to aim for the highest standards of all; for the very purity of Christ himself. Once settle for anything less – and we are backsliders! We are to set our sights on one hundred percent…. *knowing that in this life we will never attain it*. We are going to be fighters for ever.

We can live with this tension, once we understand it. Ours is a learning experience. We are wanting to please the Lord, to be like him in character and deeds. One day we shall indeed be like him, when we finally see him and are with him for ever. This very expectation spurs us on to keep co-operating with the Spirit of Christ within us:

> *But we know that when he appears, we shall be like him, for we shall see him as he is. Everyone who has this hope in him purifies himself, just as he is pure (1 John 3:2,3).*

So.... stay in the fight. There will be many occasions when we are aware of failure – but we can learn from these setbacks, and ask ourselves, *Where did I go wrong? What had I forgotten? How can I do better next time?* For we can be quite sure that there will be a next time.

Here is a second maxim:

Stay in the fellowship

Look again at 1 Peter 5:9, with its encouragement to resist the devil – 'standing firm in the faith, because you know that your brothers throughout the world are undergoing the same kind of sufferings.' The apostle Paul makes a similar point in a key Bible sentence that I learnt by heart at college:

> *No temptation has seized you except what is common to man. And God is faithful; he will not let you be tempted beyond what you can bear. But when you are tempted, he will also provide a way out so that you can stand up under it. (1 Corinthians 10:13).*

No one is alone in the difficulties, or the pressure to cave in. The Christian fellowship is there around us, to recharge both the morale and the will. We were not really meant to be battling for holiness as isolated hermits. It is as we gather around the Scriptures with our friends; as we eat together, as we unite in worship, outreach and service, that we learn the lessons of success *jointly*. Back to the words of Augustine again!

'One loving spirit sets another on fire.'

A group of loving friends can give support and encouragement when one of its members comes under immense pressure in the workplace, or from the pull of sexual temptation. An example: our hearts should go out to Christian men and women who experience a degree of same-sex attraction, yet battle courageously on for a pure lifestyle in keeping with the Scriptures. They deserve every ounce of our support – for we can be sure that they will receive none from any other quarter whatsoever.[2]

The risks increase when a Christian becomes isolated from the fellowship. Peter's danger moment, as a disciple, came when he was separated from John and the others after the arrest of Jesus. Sitting among the Lord's enemies, and challenged by some idle questioning, he denied with oaths that he had ever known his master. The disciple Thomas was the poorer for not being present at the first electric meeting between the risen Jesus and the other disciples. We get the impression that he had cut himself off from the rest. The title of Doubting Thomas might not have stuck to him if he had stayed in with his companions.

Business people, when travelling alone to a distant city, do well to e-mail or ring their fellowship group leader: "Can't be with you tonight – but here are my prayer requests!" *In the fight, we need each other.*

Here is a third maxim:

Stay in communion

I'm back at the Scripture Union house party once more as a sixteen-year-old. I'm looking forward to some tennis coaching in a few minutes, from Douglas Argyle, a Wimbledon player! Just now, however, Mr Nash is giving a talk in the library. The piano has thumped out a Christian

[2] On this and other sexual issues, see chapters 13–16 in *New Issues Facing Christians Today*, John Stott, IVP

song, which is never sung today. But its words have often come back to me:

> *Jesus my Saviour, Jesus my Saviour;*
> *Greatest of all friends he is to me.*
> *When I am lonely, I'll trust him only;*
> *Constant Companion I'll prove him to be*

'My Saviour.' The theme is taken up by the speaker now. At no point, he emphasises, will Jesus cease to be my Saviour, either in the past, present or future.

"Do you know the three 'tenses' of salvation?" he asks.

I'm not sure that I do, so I pick up my pen. It sounds like a grammar lesson.

"We have these three *tenses of salvation*," declared Mr Nash. I was all attention as a young Christian.

"I *have been saved*, initially, from the *penalty* of sin by a *crucified Saviour*."

The sound of ballpoints, scribbling frantically on paper, was almost deafening.

"Next," said our erudite speaker, "I am *being saved*, progressively, from the *power* of sin by a *living Saviour*. This goes on all through my life as a Christian."

I banged the information into my notebook, and looked up expectantly for the next point. Sure enough, it came.

"And thirdly," I heard, "I *shall be saved* finally, from the *presence* of sin altogether, by a *coming Saviour*. This occurs when I die, or when Christ returns to earth – whichever happens first."

I put down my pen with a sense of achievement. In three deft sentences Mr Nash had given us the truths of justification, sanctification and glorification. My past sins, my present battles and my future perfection in the coming glory…. why, Christ is the key to the problem of sin *all along the line*. Up to the end of my life I am dependent upon him for my salvation at every point, and – as my vision of him as risen and ascended world Saviour is enlarged – my motivation is raised accordingly. I find myself *wanting* to win. Why, I am going to see him one day!

Stay close then. Stay in communion and fellowship every day.

Had you thought of taking the Bible into every day? After all, we Christians are people of the Book. I remember walking past Starbucks Café in London's Regent Street, only to spot through the front window a colleague, Stephen Nichols, and an Asian friend sitting inside side by side. Both had pocket Bibles open in front of them, and a mug of coffee each. They smiled at me through the window. That's the style! They were having fellowship together in Christ. If you're carrying the Bible on your person into every day, the strong likelihood is that you will be referring to it at different moments, and you will be strengthened in your remembrance of the Lord, and in your communion with him.

I was exhorting fellow leaders to do the same thing, at a conference once. "If you can't afford a small Bible for your pocket or handbag, put it on your birthday list!" I urged. *"Every Christian worker should carry a Bible with them."*

The next evening at the conference, London vicar Andrew Baughen put on an end-of-day summing up video. On it we saw a spoof interviewer among conference delegates.

"May we see your pocket Bible, sir? We're the Richard Bewes pocket Bible police. That's right, sir – just a spot check! Your Bible…oh, you have it only in your *car*? I'm afraid we'll have to make a note of that….Er, Good morning, Bishop; may we see your Bible please?…."

It was an amusing little clip, but Andrew Baughen made the point. In fact, delegates were coming up to us over the following days: *You'll be glad to know, I've just got myself a pocket Bible!*

It's the Book that brings Jesus closer to us. With this reminder of him at your side, it's unlikely that you will find yourself visiting pornographer's shops, losing control of your tongue or carrying out shady business deals. Riding on public transport, or indeed sitting in a Starbucks cafeteria, we can pull out that Bible for an extra read, or to learn a Scripture verse by heart. We are people of the Book – *his* Book.

Stay in communion. If we consciously take Christ into every day, we can not only win against the world, the flesh and the devil, but we can also be living reminders to others of the life that wins.

One of the first prominent Christian leaders to emerge after the times of Christ's apostles was Ignatius. He was the second Bishop of Antioch, and was reputed to have known the apostle John. Ignatius died as a martyr under the Roman imperial rule of Trajan, the Caesar of that time, around the year AD 107.

Ignatius was so concerned to 'carry' the Lord with him into his every action, that those who knew him gave him the nickname of "The God-Bearer". And when the emperor Trajan asked him,

"Dost thou then bear the crucified One in thy heart?" Ignatius' answer was emphatic.

"Even so; for it is written, 'I will dwell in them, and walk in them, and I will be their God and they shall be my people.'"

The God-Bearer. That can be the title of any believer. When such friends of Jesus live up to this description, they can take the fight into the toughest of situations; meeting temptation and adversity head-on, and *expecting* to win – even if it costs them their lives.

14

FACING A NEW
PRE-CHRISTIAN ERA

Liz and I were travelling together on the London Underground in June 2004. Opposite us in the carriage was a young woman. A bag was on her lap. Printed on it was this message:

> *Freedom*
> *Open your mind*
> *Live the dream*
> *Go where you will*
> *Life is out there*

That roughly sums up the philosophical mindset of many people in the West today. They are not exactly *irreligious*. In fact as far back as the 1960s Marshall McLuhan, the communications whizz-kid of Toronto University, was predicting a new 'religious' age by the end of the twentieth century. He has been proved right.

Although millions of British citizens live as practical atheists, a vaguely religious outlook characterises the belief-system of many. It makes no demands in terms of moral behaviour or dedicated single-mindedness. There's something 'out there', a force, spirit-guides…. a god? You can walk into one of London's biggest stores, Selfridges in Oxford Street, and visit the vast book section there. Under *Religion*, will be found publications on Buddhist meditation, Chant and Prayer, Bhakti-Yoga, or How to Consult your Angel. *As I write, there is not a single Bible on the shelves.*

Walk on a little and visit one of the London churches. There you can pick up a magazine – *Alternatives* – with its offer of talks to be given at the church. Topics include *Lessons from an Angel; Stepping into the Boundless; Sex, Love and Tantra; and The Shaman's Rules of Power in Business and Life.* Weekend workshops are offered on such subjects as *Living Magically, Starlight in your Life and Sekhem Energy Healing.*

Such trends were beginning to surface significantly in September 1997 – in the public outpouring of grief at the death of Diana, Princess of Wales. Much of it possessed a religious flavour – though unconnected with historic Christianity; the banks of flowers, the vigils, the candle-lit shrines dedicated to the Queen of Hearts – and such comments as 'She's in another world now; she'll be looking after the children there.'

If the apostle Paul could leapfrog two millennia and make these observations for himself, he might well conclude that history is repeating itself at the present time. For, back in AD 49, his impression of the Greek capital was of a pluralistic 'religious' city:

While Paul was waiting for them in Athens, he was greatly distressed to see that the city was full of idols. So he reasoned in the synagogue with the Jews and the God-

fearing Greeks, as well as in the market-place day by day with those who happened to be there.... .....Paul then stood up in the meeting of the Areopagus and said: "Men of Athens! I see that in every way you are very religious" (Acts 17:16,17,22).

You can visit the rocky site of the Areopagus today – the small 'Hill of Ares,' the Greek god of war. It was also called 'Mars Hill', after the equivalent Roman deity. The Council that met there possessed great jurisdiction in matters of religion and morals, and was within easy walking distance of the great Parthenon temple. The words of Paul's striking sermon of Acts 17 have been carved into the side of the famous site, where the Christian faith made its historic challenge – ultimately successful – against the bewildering supermarket of religions and altars that then dominated all Europe.

The fact that Athene, Mithras, Venus, Artemis, Cybele, Osiris, Apollo, Jupiter – and a fantastic array of other deities – were all eventually to be swept into oblivion by the Christian preachers, says it all. When the Scriptures are proclaimed and taught fearlessly and clearly, we can expect society to be changed and even unified. As the historian T.R. Glover put it, "Christianity stabilises society without sterilising it." That is, provided it is real Christianity!

This has been the challenge of recent times. During the late nineteenth century a tide of destructive German teaching swept across the world of theology, undermining belief in the authority of the Scriptures. Many millions of believers around the world could have been threatened by these scholars, for few would have been academically equipped to deal with this unexpected attack. However, what held great numbers of them intact in their faith were the hymns that came out of the Moody and Sankey mission meetings. No less than eighty million copies of *Sacred Songs and Solos* were distributed around the world, and more people listened to the singing of Ira D. Sankey in the one year of 1875 than heard the works of J.S. Bach during the entire century.

But the damage was done at the level of the seminaries and universities. From there the insidious teaching drip-fed its way down to the schools, and into great numbers of churches. It was not until the second half of the twentieth century that orthodox and evangelical scholarship had rallied sufficiently to challenge the liberals' attacks on creedal, biblical belief. Church leadership at the top became severely affected, and to this day it cannot be said that it has really recovered.

The arrival in the West of 'New Age' teaching, with its human-centred emphasis on subjective experience and nature-based religion, found little to combat it. Hence the erosion – in the media, in education and in much church life – of the New Testament brand of Gospel teaching that 'turned the world upside down' proclaimed by Paul and his friends throughout the Roman empire. Today many of the former 'gods' are resurfacing, albeit under new names, and we find ourselves rubbing shoulders in the philosophical market-place with a whole number of what are, in fact, very old ghosts!

The story has nearly gone full circle; *we are back in Athens again.*

All this is a clear demonstration that no generation can rest content on the achievements of its predecessors. It can be painful to realise that, in our own turn, we are being called upon to fight the same battles all over again – for the inspiration of the Bible, the centrality of the cross, the deity of Jesus, justification and the new birth, the sexual ethic and the call to evangelism. It is not that we are without evidence of unprecedented church growth in a great many parts of the world. But the lesson across much of the West is stark.

To lose confidence in the Scriptures and to cease to 'contend for the faith that was once for all entrusted to the saints' (Jude 3) is to provide a perfect exercise in how to wreck a church. Who would ever wish to be part of a church whose message was muted and hesitant? It is little wonder that such churches rapidly lose their members and that the resulting religious vacuum is filled by incoming alien belief-systems. Wherever the apostolic Gospel is preached there is life and growth. Wherever it is compromised and blunted, decay and death are the certain result.

Rise to the challenge. Accept a call as you read this page. Many in western circles are fond of talking about today's 'post-Christian era'. Actually, it is more exciting than that. Across all of Europe and in much of North America and the Antipodes *we are facing a new pre-Christian era.* There is a generation around us that has never heard the good news. International students arriving in London will sometimes admit that they have never heard of Jesus.

The novelty of the Gospel

Back to the Areopagus! Acts chapter 17 portrays Paul, with the imposing Parthenon right behind him, as he engages with the cleverest thinkers in Athens. *Jesus?* Rising from the dead? The appointed judge of the whole world?

They had no idea what Paul was talking about. It was completely new to them, even a little amusing.

So it is today.

> *A group of Epicurean and Stoic philosophers began to dispute with him. Some of them asked, "What is this babbler trying to say?" Others remarked, "He seems to be advocating foreign gods." They said this because Paul was preaching the good news about Jesus and the resurrection. Then they took him and brought him to a meeting of the Areopagus, where they said to him, "May we know what this new teaching is that you are presenting?…" (Acts 17:18,19).*

New teaching? It was much more than that. Paul and his friends had not come to Athens to enunciate a new religious principle, or to promote an idea that no one had yet heard of. Here was no philosophy or self-help programme. Something, rather, had *happened*. Heaven had *spoken* and Someone had *come*! A death and resurrection had taken place, and the world could never be the same again. Paul and Barnabas, Luke, Timothy and Silas had come in with an Announcement.

Those Christian messengers gave no indication of fighting a defensive rearguard action. While of course we should be familiar with the currents of modern thought around us, I do not read of Barnabas saying to Paul, "Our job is just to *listen* to the Athenians; we must try to *understand* them." They already understood them well enough – and they came in, without apology, setting the pace from the very start.

We have some distinct advantages, as we witness to Christ today. In a pre-Christian society you can come straight in with a clean sheet! In the nineteenth century most of English society thought of itself as 'Christian'; it was only with difficulty that the defences of nominal belief could be broken down. Those with whom we now share our faith are very different. And they are not overburdened by unwelcome 'baggage', left over from previous unfortunate experiences with the church; frequently they will have had no experience of church life at all.

In the well-known *Christianity Explored* course for enquirers, we feel no need to put on, as our first session, a defence of the Bible as the inspired Word of God. There is no need to. Without apology we simply bring out Bibles for every course member and have them opened from the first day. Our reasoning is that *the Scriptures will speak for themselves*; that the Holy Spirit will use the Bible's inherent life-changing power to lead men and women to God. And this happens.

Certainly there is increasing 'containment' of the church in our present time. Ours is a society that is deliberately setting aside its Christian heritage in favour of an all-comers' approach to religion. Anything is believable; this presents us with a set of difficulties. But we are at least permitted to set out our stall! We are jostling, like Paul in Athens, with Hindus, Buddhists, Sikhs and pagans, and we must have the confidence to set out the message of Christ as brilliant good news – as fresh to our fellow-citizens as it was when Augustine came to the shores of Britain in AD 597.

The message has a cutting edge; it results in a call for decision. The Areopagus address ended by punching a hole through the defences of Paul's listeners – for the apostle ended with a final challenge of universal judgement (Acts 17:31). They had never heard anything like it before, and some of them became Christians that very day. Share Christ in the power of the Holy Spirit – and people will always be aware of the novelty of the Gospel!

The networking of the Gospel

It was amazing. They had no media to speak of, no favours that were shown them by the Roman imperial power, no money, no premises and no equipment. How can the effectiveness of that early Christian network be explained?

They did – of course – have the advantage of the Greek language that was common across the whole Roman world. That meant that there were no translation problems as they crossed border after border. It was natural that all the general communication was going to be in Greek – including the writing of the New Testament.

They also had the Roman roads. They were the equivalent of the Blue Ridge Parkway in North Carolina, or Britain's famous M1. The message of *sins dealt with at the Cross*, and *death defeated on the Third Day* was gossiped all along the great *Via Egnatia*, that ran from the Adriatic in the West, right through to Constantinople in the East. But that still does not fully explain the miraculous spread of the message of Jesus.

The answer is that he had pledged himself to be with his friends 'to the very end of the age' (Matthew 28:19). It was not up to them; it was up to the promised Spirit to give guidance and impetus to the task. Luke records of the first missionary journey that 'they tried to enter Bithynia, *but the Spirit of Jesus would not allow them to*' (Acts 16:7). Yes, he was in charge! We call the book of Acts 'The Acts of the Apostles', but a more accurate title would be 'The Acts of the Holy Spirit'.

It was supremely through prayer that they drew upon this power. Look where you will in the book of Acts; we keep reading of their praying – and things happened. It is invariably so in the history of great spiritual awakenings. I have tried to make the point elsewhere that the centre of prayer is not us, but God.[1] Once we suppose ourselves to be in the driving seat as we call upon the Lord, then our prayers are little better than age-old attempts at magic, in which human beings would try to bend spiritual powers to bring about their own will. Real prayer takes place when God is in the driving seat, and when his servants, in obedience to his summons, bring people, and the work of his kingdom before him, leaving the final issues with him, as the trusted Father. Prayer is God's chosen way of involving us in the fulfilling of his will. We pray; he works!

It is surely because of the power of prayer that the temptation is so strong to neglect it. Prayer is usually the first thing to go out of the window. If there is no prayer meeting in your church, you need not make a great scene about it. Simply begin to pray yourself. Then recruit a prayer partner. Make it a triplet! Make it a breakfast! And what do you pray for? Open up a dossier on some country or Christian organisation that you have a concern for. Newspaper cuttings, missionary magazine snippets, photographs, letters – all can help to inform our prayers. Praying for one's church, praying for family and friends, praying for people who have yet to follow Christ…. we can build up a list, and pray through the month with its help.

---

[1] *Talking about Prayer*, by Richard Bewes, Christian Focus Publications, http://www.christianfocus.com

What is happening? Why, we are creating a network of the Gospel. How did Paul ever manage to remember those strings of names that he was greeting at the end of his letters? *They were in his prayers* – frequently.

Our critics will sometimes wonder how we could ever embark upon such a 'narrow' group as the church. But it is they who are the narrow ones. To become a Christian stretches your borders to the ends of the world. It is an education to go to a proper prayer meeting, to a half-night of prayer! That way you can be spending time in half a dozen countries *as effectively as if you were there in person*. There is a great network of the Gospel out there, and we are a part of it!

The necessity of the Gospel

Is it a little unnecessary to labour this point? Not at all. Without the Gospel of Christ, all we are left with is an idolatrous community, which in some circles must be interpreted as the 'me' culture. When I was a boy, I was taught that self-centredness was not a good thing to pursue. Now, it appears in some quarters, we are being led to believe that you *should* be self-centred. If, indeed, society is left to itself, that is the likely direction that it will take. The historian H.M. Gwatkin comments upon the early Church's effect upon its surrounding culture:

> *This change from self to unself as the spring of human action, is the greatest revolution which the world has seen.*[2]

But there is more to it than this. Without the good news of Christ, there is only judgement and eternal

---

[2] *Early Church History*, MacMillan 1909, Vol I, page 225

death awaiting the whole human race. There have been many attempts to provide a system, a religion by which humanity can climb up to the Infinite. As we have said earlier, the Bible turns the whole quest on its head. It is God who has been seeking us out from our fall onwards, in the person of Jesus. He is the universal, the *only* Saviour. *There are many roads to Christ! But he is the only way to the Father* (John 14:6). This is not a narrow appeal. Christ is big enough to fill the universe; he is broad enough to take in every man, woman, boy or girl from every conceivable culture, who will come to the cross to receive him.

We are so concerned that men and women find forgiveness at his feet that, if necessary, martyrs have given their lives in order that others might hear. Paul and the other apostles suffered unimaginably in the cause of the Christ they followed. Christians suffer for two main reasons; firstly, because we are following a leader who has suffered ahead of us, and we are to follow in his footsteps, and secondly because he has chosen adversity as the pathway by which discipleship may be strengthened. [3]

Ours is a blood and thunder faith, and our prayer must be that when suffering comes our way as disciples of Jesus (and he tells us to expect it), we may be able to count ourselves as honoured by the Lord, and in truly noble company! Too often, Christians in hard times have hoped that it would not be too long before they were relieved, and therefore able to get back to 'the normal Christian life'. Then they came to realise that, as far as the New Testament

---

[3] For a fuller statement on Christian suffering, see the author's book on the kingdom of God, *The Stone That Became a Mountain*, Christian Focus, ch. 9.

is concerned, suffering *is* the normal Christian life.

It is in no glib way that we reaffirm the old saying that the blood of the martyrs is the seed of the church. Some of my own African friends have died, in the urgency of their desire to make Christ known. Such is 'the necessity of the Gospel', and we are humbled to the dust by such commitment.

The nerve of the Gospel

The tendency in a pre-Christian era, is to adapt the message a little when the heat is on; to tone it down and make it more 'acceptable'. But it is the way of death. We are not to adapt to the spirit of the age, but to hold our nerve and challenge it.

Think of the Wesley brothers. They came onto the scene in Britain when spiritual life was at a low ebb. They were both ministers before they had been converted! Then, having been awoken by the message of the Bible, they made the resolve to change the course of history. It was a horseback existence. The clods flew, riots broke out in such places as Wednesbury, and what John called 'Wicked Wigan'. If they were tempted to give up, we have no record of it. The churches were closed to their preaching, and they took to the fields. Bans were placed upon them; yet they continued in their ministry. John did the preaching – forty thousand sermons in all – and Charles produced the hymns, seven thousand of them, when he had finished. And, as one writer has commented, they produced not a religion *for* the people, but a religion *of* the people.

The plain historical fact is that when a strong nerve is called for; when outreach in mission is the priority, when bold actions are to be taken, it is the single individuals and private initiatives that get the work done. Very rarely are the exciting exploits undertaken and carried through by appointed committees or by the denominational leadership. Officialdom may eventually – even reluctantly – endorse a piece of Christian enterprise and give it the required stamp of approval, but it is the non-institutional people who usually get the idea off the ground and the website set up!

This is not to decry church officialdom and central structures. If our leaders have their wits about them, they know a good thing when they see it, and will give it public recognition. Nevertheless, if the officials of the Wesley era had had their way, we would, in Britain, have missed a time of remarkable revival in the eighteenth century.

A new pre-Christian era. What will happen next? That question must have been asked when the city of Rome was sacked in a single day, on August 24th, AD 410. Augustine was asked about this, far away in Carthage. 'What now? What about poor Rome?' Nerves were shattered.

Rome? queried Augustine. Who was interested in preserving *Rome*? It was not all over, insisted the 56 year-old leader. There was another city to be interested in, and it was the City of God. People were wondering what the next thing was to be? Why, the next thing was Christ.

People will ask the same question again in our own generation. Look at the things that are happening! What are we to do? What can we expect? What's coming?

If we are followers of Jesus, we are very honoured and blessed to be among the precursors of what is coming next!

IT'S GOING TO BE CHRIST

15

THE CALL FROM THE SHORE

Breakfast….on the beach….with Jesus Christ! It's enough to last anyone an entire lifetime.

And so it proved to be. There were seven of them present that morning by the Lake of Galilee. Yes, we can call it a lake. Matthew, Mark and John all refer to it as a 'sea' – and to them it was, for it was the biggest stretch of water that they were acquainted with. Seven miles across, twelve miles long. But Luke was an international traveller; he had been with Paul in the Mediterranean. *Galilee a sea? Well, okay. But in my Gospel book I'm calling it the Lake of Galilee!*

They were eating tilapia fish by the water's edge. All along that great fissure on the earth's surface – running right down into the great Rift Valley of East Africa – there is a string of lakes, and nearly all of them are stocked with those distinctive chubby fish. The Lake of Galilee is one of them.

"Is this tilapia?" I ask my African hosts by Rwanda's Lake Kivu. They nod their confirmation.

"Eating this gives us an extra bond with Jesus," I confide. "He's had tilapia too!" Our eyes meet joyfully across the table.

There is something very reassuring in the simple scene by the lake on that post-Easter morning. Taking place there is the birth of a mighty world-wide adventure that has not ended yet. It all begins with the kind of breakfast party that would not be uncommon today on Sydney's Bondi Beach. Authentic first-hand witness is stamped all over this glowing account:

> *When they landed, they saw a fire of burning coals there with fish on it, and some bread. Jesus said to them, "Bring some of the fish you have just caught." Simon Peter climbed aboard and dragged the net ashore. It was full of large fish, 153, but even with so many the net was not torn. Jesus said to them, "Come and have breakfast" (John 21:9-12).*

The frustrating night of failure for the fishing party; the stranger on the shore in the misty dawn; the distant shout – "How are you doing, guys?"

There's the little detail that – as they were instructed from the beach – it was to be on the *right* side of the boat that the net should be thrown out this time. The amazing catch…. Peter's hundred yard splash to shore…. the charcoal fire and 'large' tilapia fish….the typical action of fishermen in counting the catch – how we love the Bible, with its teeming stories!

Simon Peter is about to receive his commission as a leader in the universal church that is coming into being. There are just seven present; Nathaniel, Peter, James, John and Thomas – and two others, unidentified. There would have been room in the boat for all of them, for – if the first century Galilean fishing boat excavated in 1986 is anything to go by – it would have been twenty-eight feet long.

It is not only the once-crucified leader who will become known on every continent. These associates by the fireside will also become household names.

Look at Peter, his tunic still damp with lake water. He doesn't know it – but great cathedrals and even towns and cities are going to be called after him in years to come. And one day he will be a martyr; Jesus makes this plain to him (vv. 18 and 19), while the charcoal embers are still red.

Look over there at John. The book that is to be written by this member of the Israeli fishing industry is going to be pored over and discussed by the best theological brains that the church can muster. John's Gospel will become the biggest single item of literature ever distributed and read.[1]

Can you see Thomas? He is unaware of it right now, but he's going to end up in India, and millions of Indians are going to adopt his name one day. Yes, and there is *James*, folding up the fishing net. He's not going to end up anywhere; within weeks he will be finishing his days at the hands of Herod Agrippa's execution squad – it's recorded for us in Acts 12:2.

St John's College…. St James Square…. St Petersburg…. St Thomas' Hospital – I can't easily think of any Herod Street, or Nero University! The mighty Caesar had a haircut and a salad named after him, but as often as not his name – as Andrew Knowles has pointed out – is reserved usually for the family dog. [2] Just one of the changes Jesus makes!

---

[1] John's Gospel with Anne Graham-Lotz, Paul Blackham and Richard Bewes; *Book by Book* video/dvd series www.allsouls.org For USA, www.visionvideo.com

[2] *The Way Out*, Collins 1977, page 38

And here, with the 153 fish still to be counted on the shore, the thought must have occurred to Peter, *Isn't this where we came in?* It was like playing back the video. The call by a supposed non-expert to let down the net just 'one more time' – resulting in a catch big enough to get itself into the Bible – why, it had happened before, right at the beginning in Luke chapter 5. Christ's words, spoken then, would have been etched in Peter's memory,

"From now on you will be catching not fish but men."

So much has happened by the time of this second great catch. The miracles, stories and lessons learned. The controversies; the arrest, trial and crucifixion of Peter's master. The anguished memory of his three-fold denial by a fireside is about to be cancelled out by a three-times repeated question, put to Peter by the Lord,

"Do you love me?"

Significantly, *they are at a fireside again*. It was painful for the big fisherman, and he would have remembered his bombast before Jesus' arrest,

"Even if all fall away on account of you, I never will."

Now he is just able to stammer the words out,

"Lord, you know all things; you know that I love you."

Here is not only a reinstatement of a failed disciple; this is a recommissioning – with its fresh charge in addition to that of 'catching men'. From now on Jesus also requires Peter to

'

Feed my lambs….take care of my sheep….feed my sheep' (*John 21:15-18*).

As the Bible commentator B.F. Westcott observes,

"The fisher's work is followed by the shepherd's work." [3]

Is it providential that John, the eye-witness writer, never gives his readers the identity of the 'two other disciples' (v. 2)? The implication might otherwise have been that there was no room for anybody else's name to be included in the circle of Christ's intimates.

But no. It could have been your name there. Isn't this where *you* came in? At some point did you hear the voice of the Son of God calling you from the Gospel shoreline? And if so, where did it happen? In church? At a mission event? From early days in the family? Through a friend's challenge? Cast your mind back to that occasion and time, when forgiveness and the gift of the indwelling Spirit joined you to the friends of Jesus with whom you now share a place in the boat!

What has he got for you now? Whatever daily work or situation may be ours, all can take an active share in Peter's role – both of fishing and shepherding. Most are not called to go 'full time' in the paid ministry of the church – although this came to me when I was six or seven – before I had even made my decision at Mr Nash's meeting. For me it was not a call from the shore, but a call on the veranda at breakfast time in sunny Kenya. A discussion was going on at table as to what we three boys would do when we were grown up. Elizabeth my sister was only just born. Older brother Peter was emphatic:

"I'm going to be a doctor." Later he became one.

---

[3] *The Speaker's Commentary*, John Murray Publishers, London, 1880

"I'm going to do business," chimed in Michael. And it happened!

All eyes turned on me.

"What about you, Richard?"

I looked down, fidgeted and became silent. For the life of me I couldn't think of anything. Then my mother said something that I was to remember for ever.

"I think that Richard might one day be a church minister."

The conversation changed. I said nothing, but inwardly my mother's words settled it. *That's it; I'm to be a church minister.* Nothing else ever replaced this conviction. The Scripture Union house party later brought everything to a personal decision about following Christ as Saviour and Lord. Then, through Billy Graham at Harringay Arena, the call to church leadership was confirmed and underlined. It was like a drumbeat, night after night during three months of amazing meetings. "You are going to be doing this yourself, for the rest of your life."

And what about you? We are not to be looking over our shoulder at the path and destiny of others, or to become carbon copies of Christians whom we admire. We are to be uniquely ourselves. Even there on the beach, Peter was momentarily deflected from his own calling, by the sight of John nearby:

> *Peter turned and saw that the disciple whom Jesus loved was following them…. When Peter saw him, he asked, "Lord, what about him?" Jesus answered, "If I want him to remain alive until I return, what is that to you? You must follow me" (John 21:20-22).*

How can we make our so-short stay on this world as significant and effective as possible? The answer is by strengthening our sense of responsibility to Christ our leader in everything we are touching. We are here for him. We may indeed be in medicine, as my brother Peter was. We may enter business as my brother Michael did. We may become immersed in church work as my sister did, in her marriage to one of Christ's ordained pastors. We may find ourselves in the world of the creative arts like Liz, my wife. We may not be in paid work at all.

But to be a part of the active life of the church is to be in the boat, along with the apostolic fellowship. We are here for Jesus and his church. It is a call, and it was so for Peter.

Whose call, but Christ's call?
If it wasn't for a sense of call, every one of us might fold up! It is often hard and difficult, following Christ. Only those with a sense of call will still be in the boat when the balloon goes up, the revolution takes place, when a church becomes wracked with division and error.

Whose word, but Christ's word?
'*Feed* my sheep', he had said. Teaching a family, teaching one's friends, teaching a student seminar, a class at church, or in a prison cell; the servant of the Lord is to see to it that the word that is shared for life and eternity is none other than *Christ's* word, and not one's own. The power that brings forgiveness and new life can only come from one source!

Whose flock, but Christ's flock?

'*My* lambs….*My* sheep.' It is a solemn charge. Whether you are as a working person introducing others to the wonder of the kingdom of God, a house-group leader, a church council member, an ordained pastor or a praying parent, the responsibility – to be true to our calling and to be faithful to such flock as is ours – is given from the very top.

It was never *your* flock, but his – with the incentive given to us by Peter himself, later in his New Testament letter:

> *And when the Chief Shepherd appears, you will receive the crown of glory that will never fade away (1 Peter 5:4).*

Do you love me? We can almost smell the tilapia grilling on that little charcoal fire, as we hear the words reaching out to us from the Galilean shore. We will make it our aim to please him – for no other reason than we love him, who first loved us.

A BELIEVER IS SURELY A LOVER, YEA,
OF ALL LOVERS THE MOST IN LOVE!

Other Books of Interest
from
Richard Bewes

_____

RICHARD BEWES

THE TOP
100
QUESTIONS

Biblical Answers to Popular Questions

Plus - Explanations of
50 Difficult Bible Passages

The Top 100 Questions

Biblical Answers to Popular Questions.
Plus 50 Difficult Passages

Richard Bewes

As a pastor of a vibrant city church in the heart of London, Richard Bewes faces tricky questions about his faith on almost a daily basis. This book is a compilation of his Top 100 Questions, asked by people from all walks of life and religious belief, along with an appendix dealing with difficult Bible passages and questions that can arise from them.

The answers Richard offers are not pat answers to outwit the questioner, but rather, he seeks to give clear, biblical advice to genuine questions.

'...the accumulated wisdom and illustration from decades of mulling over some very difficult questions - wonderfully distilled down to the key points.'

Rico Tice, Author, Christianity Explored

'...gives deeply thought-out, carefully informed answers to many of the questions most troublesome to contemporary humanity.'

Dallas Willard, Author, 'The Divine Conspiracy'

'...I'm already planning who I could send copies of the book to when it's published.'

Peter Maiden, Operation Mobilisation

ISBN 1-85792-680-3

WORDS THAT CIRCLED THE WORLD

A Christian's response to 13 quotations that have shaped our times

RICHARD BEWES

'a rich blend of insight, sanity, wisdom and humour'
John Stott

Is that it?
I have a dream.
Get up out of your seats.
God himself couldn't sink this ship.
Power grows out of the barrel of a gun.
...one small step for a man...
...a queen in people's hearts.
Our city will never be the same.
The moment the alive resolves.
I did not have sex with that woman.
I have in my hand a piece of paper.
I've been on a calendar, but never on time.
If you can meet with Triumph and Disaster...

Words that Circled the World

*A Christian response to 13 quotations
that define our age*

Richard Bewes weaves some of the best known quotes of our era into a remarkable book. Through these well known statements he is able to explore what motivates the modern mind and contrasts it with the wisdom of the Christian message. This unique book enables you to understand why the Christian faith is such a radical alternative in the post-modern world.

"It is well conceived, well researched and well written. Readers will find in it, as I have done, a rich blend of insight, sanity, wisdom and humour, with Jesus Christ himself always at the centre."

John Stott

Some of the quotes included are -
'I have in my hand a piece of paper' – Neville Chamberlain
'I have a dream' – Martin Luther King
'That's one small step for a man one giant leap for mankind'
– Neil Armstrong
'I'd like to be a queen in people's hearts' –

Diana, Princess of Wales
'I'm going to ask you to get up out of your seat' – Billy Graham
'I did not have sex with that woman' – President Bill Clinton
'To those who say that our city will never be the same I say, "You are right. It will be better"' - Mayor Rudi Guiliani

RICHARD BEWES

THE
STONE
THAT BECAME A
MOUNTAIN

Getting it RIGHT about the Kingdom of God
'One of the most important books I have read' David Suchet

The Stone that became a Mountain

Getting it right about the Kingdom of God

Richard Bewes

'In today's changing world, where nations rise and fall, leaders come and go, thrones are occupied and emptied, treaties are made and broken, and life itself seems so fragile, The Stone that became a Mountain is the telescope that brings into focus the unchanging, transcending kingdom of God. Well done, Richard Bewes!'

Anne Graham-Lotz of Angel Ministries
(Billy Graham's daughter)

'The Kingdom of God is a non negotiable in Christian understanding. Have you grasped it? Nothing else so clearly shapes Christian thinking. This is the book - laced with vivid illustration - to explain this essential Christian truth.'

Rico Tice, Author, Christianity Explored

Beginning with the prophet Daniel's glowing imagery of the stone that grew into a mountain, Richard Bewes has come up with a colourful - and vital - presentation of the biggest thing there is; the kingdom that outlives and outlasts everything else in sight.

'Get the teaching wrong,' says Richard, 'and you land yourself in a traffic-jam of errors which will affect just about everything you ever do or touch. But get it right, and you'll be able to hold your own - and win - in the face of the false ideologies and alien teachings that are flooding our world in the twenty-first century.'

ISBN 1-85792-714-1

Christian Focus Publications

Our mission statement –

STAYING FAITHFUL

In dependence upon God we seek to help make His infallible Word, the Bible, relevant. Our aim is to ensure that the Lord Jesus Christ is presented as the only hope to obtain forgiveness of sin, live a useful life and look forward to heaven with Him.

REACHING OUT

Christ's last command requires us to reach out to our world with His gospel. We seek to help fulfill that by publishing books that point people towards Jesus and help them develop a Christ-like maturity. We aim to equip all levels of readers for life, work, ministry and mission.

Books in our adult range are published in three imprints.

Christian Focus contains popular works including biographies, commentaries, basic doctrine and Christian living. Our children's books are also published in this imprint.

Mentor focuses on books written at a level suitable for Bible College and seminary students, pastors, and other serious readers. The imprint includes commentaries, doctrinal studies, examination of current issues and church history.

Christian Heritage contains classic writings from the past.

Christian Focus Publications, Ltd
Geanies House, Fearn,
Ross-shire, IV20 1TW, Scotland, United Kingdom
info@christianfocus.com

www.christianfocus.com